Rain Forests
of the
World

Volume 6
Indonesia–Manatee

MARSHALL CAVENDISH
NEW YORK • LONDON • TORONTO • SYDNEY

Marshall Cavendish Corporation
99 White Plains Road
Tarrytown, New York
10591-9001

Website: www.marshallcavendish.com

Consulting Editors: Rolf E. Johnson, Nathan E. Kraucunas

Contributing Authors: Theresa Greenaway, Jill Bailey, Michael Chinery, Malcolm Penny, Mike Linley, Philip Steele, Chris Oxlade, Ken Preston-Mafham, Rod Preston-Mafham, Clare Oliver, Don Birchfield

Discovery Books
    Managing Editor: Paul Humphrey
    Project Editor: Gianna Williams
    Text Editor: Valerie Weber
    Designer: Ian Winton
    Cartographer: Stefan Chabluk
    Illustrators: Jim Channell, Stuart Lafford, Christian Webb

Marshall Cavendish
    Editor: Marian Armstrong
    Editorial Director: Paul Bernabeo

(cover) Amazon water lily

Editor's Note: Many systems of dating have been used by different cultures throughout history. *Rain Forests of the World* uses B.C.E. (Before Common Era) and C.E. (Common Era) instead of B.C. (Before Christ) and A.D. (Anno Domini, "In the Year of Our Lord") out of respect for the diversity of the world's peoples.

The publishers would like to thank the following for their permission to reproduce photographs:
300 Christer Fredriksson/Bruce Coleman, 301 Gerard Lacz/Frank Lane Picture Agency, 302 & 303 Alain Compost/Bruce Coleman, 304 R. Wilmshurst/FLPA, 305 G. I. Bernard/Oxford Scientific Films, 306 Ken Preston-Mafham/Premaphotos Wildlife, 307 M. P. L. Fogden/Bruce Coleman, 308 Ken Preston-Mafham/Premaphotos Wildlife, 309 Gunter Ziesler/Bruce Coleman, 312 P. J. De Vries/Oxford Scientific Films, 313 Gerald S. Cubitt/Bruce Coleman, 314 Alastair Macewen/Oxford Scientific Films, 315 Ken Preston-Mafham/Premaphotos Wildlife, 316 Bruce Coleman, 317 Corbis, 319 & 320 Bill Leimbach/South American Pictures, 321 Tony Morrison/South American Pictures, 322 Kevin Schafer/Natural History Photographic Agency, 323 Stephen Dalton/NHPA, 324 Katie Atkinson/Oxford Scientific Films, 325 Martin Harvey/NHPA, 326 Roine Magnusson/Bruce Coleman, 327 Rod Williams/Bruce Coleman, 328 Ken Preston-Mafham/Premaphotos Wildlife, 329 Gunter Ziesler/Bruce Coleman, 331 John Brown/Oxford Scientific Films, 332 Kim Taylor/Bruce Coleman, 333 Alain Compost/Bruce Coleman, 334 Ken Preston-Mafham/Premaphotos Wildlife, 335 Jany Sauvanet/NHPA, 336 Stephen Dalton/NHPA, 338 Alain Compost/Bruce Coleman, 339 Robin Bush/Oxford Scientific Films, 340 David Woodfall/NHPA, 342 & 343 Martin Harvey/NHPA, 344 Alain Compost/Bruce Coleman, 345 Malcolm Penny, 346 & 347 Gerald S. Cubitt/Bruce Coleman, 348 Gerard Lacz/FLPA, 349 David Haring/Oxford Scientific Films, 350 & 351 Corbis, 352 Joe McDonald/Bruce Coleman, 353 Michael Fodgen/Oxford Scientific Films, 354 Carlos Sanchez/Oxford Scientific Films, 355 Kevin Schafer/NHPA, 356 Alain Compost/Bruce Coleman, 357 Daniel J. Cox/Oxford Scientific Films

Library of Congress Cataloging-in-Publication Data
Rain forests of the world.
              v. cm.
        Includes bibliographical references and index.
        Contents: v. 1. Africa-bioluminescence—v. 2. Biomass-clear-cutting — v. 3. Climate and weather-emergent — v. 4. Endangered species-food web — v. 5. Forest fire-iguana — v.6. Indonesia-manatee — v. 7. Mangrove forest-orangutan — v. 8. Orchid-red panda — v. 9. Reforestation-spider — v. 10. Squirrel-Yanomami people — v. 11. Index.
            ISBN 0-7614-7254-1 (set)
            1. Rain forests—Encyclopedias. 1. Marshall Cavendish Corporation.
        QH86 .R39 2002
        578.734—dc21

    ISBN 0-7614-7254-1 (set)
    ISBN 0-7614-7260-6 (vol. 6)

Printed and bound in Italy

07 06 05 04 03 02   6 5 4 3 2 1

Contents

Indonesia

Indonesia is a land of superlatives. Consisting of hundreds of islands spread out across a tropical sea, the distance from one end to the other of this vast country is about the same as from New York to Los Angeles. The original vegetation covering many of the islands, including the largest ones of Sumatra and Borneo, was tropical rain forest. From central Java eastward, the islands become progressively drier, so that Komodo and Flores are covered in a dry scrub. However, farther east the climate becomes wetter again, so the easternmost islands of Sulawesi,

KEY FACTS

● Inch for inch, Indonesia ranks as one of the most biodiverse countries in the world.

● About 1,500 species of birds live in Indonesia; approximately 400 of these are found nowhere else in the world.

● More than 530 species of mammals live in Indonesia.

● Indonesia is home to the world's largest variety of palms.

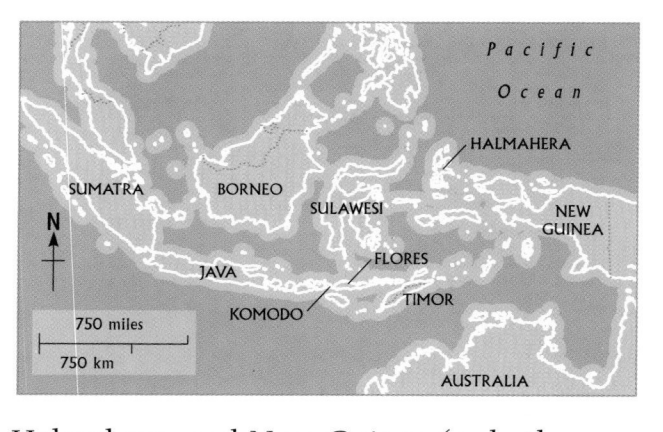

Halmahera, and New Guinea (only the western half of which is Indonesian) are covered in wet tropical forest.

Indonesia is unusual in that it forms a bridge between two distinct biological zones. Animals and plants typical of tropical Asia inhabit the western islands. The more eastern islands show a gradual change to a flora and fauna that still includes typical Asian types but also begins to include species typical of Australia and New Guinea. The line between these regions is called Wallace's line after Alfred Wallace, an English naturalist who first identified the

The rain forest clinging to the sides of the Bohorok River gorge in Sumatra forms one edge of the massive Gunung Leuser National Park.

IN FOCUS

The Long-Tailed Macaque

The highly successful long-tailed macaque (muh-KAK) is common throughout much of the region, even in densely populated areas with little remaining forest and a patchwork of cultivated fields. It can be very tame, taking food from a person's hand, but can turn nasty if someone tries to stop it from getting what it wants. It can swim and dive with ease. It is sometimes called the crab-eating macaque because of its habit of catching crabs in the mangrove swamps that fringe much of the coasts. When on the move, the female carries her baby slung upside down beneath her body so that she can leap from tree to tree relatively unhindered.

phenomenon in 1858. Islands such as Sulawesi that contain a mixture of both Asian and Australian types have an exceptionally rich range of wildlife. In Sulawesi, typically Asian animals such as macaques live side by side with cuscuses, marsupials closely related to kangaroos.

All of Indonesia lies well within the tropical zone, so temperatures are always warm and change little throughout the year, except on the higher mountains. Rainfall over the wettest forests typically reaches more than 72 inches (1,830 mm) per year, often falling during spectacular thunderstorms. The climate, the large amounts of forest, and an enormous geographical spread combine to make Indonesia one of the world's so-called megadiversity countries. Only the Amazonian region of South America can boast similarly high biodiversity within a given area.

Deforestation

Unfortunately much of Indonesia's biological wealth is rapidly being lost as huge areas of forest are cleared every day for logging, farming, mining, and creating huge plantations of rubber, oil palm, and coconut trees. Much of Java has been intensively cultivated for many hundreds of years, so the few remaining patches of forest are now isolated on mountains or in nature reserves.

Since the 1980s, the previously unspoiled forests of Sumatra and Borneo have been cleared at an alarming rate, much of it as a result of the Indonesian government's policy of transmigration. Transmigration involves moving people from overcrowded islands such as Java to the less populated islands of Sumatra and Borneo. Once the forest has been felled for farming, the newcomers' inexperience in sustainable farming techniques has in many places led to a rapid soil exhaustion. Crop yields gradually decrease, so people eventually abandon the farm plots. Such exhausted sites are slow to return to forest, since pioneer plants have difficulty getting established on the poor soils, swept bare and packed hard by heavy tropical downpours.

The long, bulbous nose of the male proboscis monkey is probably the strangest and most easily recognized feature of any primate species. When alarmed, the male produces a loud honking noise.

Animals of Indonesia

Some of the larger animals live in certain areas of Indonesia but not others; their distribution is unusual. Tigers still prowl the forests in Sumatra and Java but have never managed to reach nearby Borneo, which would provide plenty of prey and thick forest. The orangutan roams parts of Borneo and Sumatra but has never lived on nearby Java or in peninsular Malaysia. Sumatra's and Borneo's orangutans are even slightly different from each other; thus they are divided into two distinct subspecies. Indonesia as a whole is incredibly rich in primates, with a massive total of at least 29 species, 21 of which are found nowhere else. Many of these are restricted to small islands where they could easily be wiped out by large-scale logging or farming. The remarkable island of Sulawesi alone is home to seven kinds of macaques, none of which live elsewhere.

In Sumatra, Thomas's leaf monkey survives well in developed areas and will even enter houses in search of food. However, the proboscis (pruh-BAH-sus) monkey is much less adaptable; it lives only in mangrove and rain forest areas in Borneo. This strange monkey is rapidly becoming rarer as its habitat disappears.

Indonesia is home to two kinds of rhinoceroses. The rare Sumatran rhino is about half the size of the even rarer Javan rhino. The Javan rhino weighs up to 3,000 pounds (1,350 kg) and grows to between 4½ and 5½ feet (1.4 and 1.7 m) tall. Both species require large undisturbed areas of rain forest, which are now becoming scarce.

Several kinds of deer also graze in the forests, including the tiny, pencil-legged lesser mouse deer and the much larger rusa, which used to exist in huge herds of 50,000 or more. The rusa is now much rarer, although still quite widespread. The banteng is a relative of our domestic cattle. Once common, its population has become much reduced, and it is best seen in various reserves in southwestern Java.

On the island of Sulawesi live two kinds of dwarf buffalo, called anoas, one in the

IN FOCUS

Leaping Tarsiers

The smallest of Indonesia's primates are the two species of tarsiers (TAHR-see-uhrs), one found on Sulawesi and the other (pictured below eating insect prey) on Sumatra and Borneo. These tiny, insect-eating, large-eyed primates jump from tree to tree as if propelled by powerful springs. Their huge eyes give excellent night vision as the nocturnal tarsiers move swiftly around in the dark forest understory. They spend their daylight hours in family groups in hollow trees.

mountains and one in the lowlands. These look like a cross between a cow and an antelope. Wary animals, they are difficult to find in the wild. Like many animals on Sulawesi, people hunt them for their meat.

The largest mammal of the Indonesian forest is the Asian elephant, which is finding survival increasingly difficult. As the forest is reduced to isolated patches, the elephants run short of food and raid nearby plantations. This causes conflict with the local farmers, who naturally want to protect their vital crops—especially sugarcane and oil palm, both of which are regarded by the elephants as particularly tasty snacks.

Indonesia's National Parks

Indonesia has some large, superb national parks, although the money to administer them properly and to fully protect their special wildlife is not always available. People often poach rare animals for food or for the black market, and they illegally log the forest in some parks.

One of the biggest and most impressive of the protected areas is the Gunung Leuser National Park in Sumatra. With an area of about 3,900 square miles (10,000 km^2), it is one of the largest parks in Asia. It is home to many of the most endangered Asian animals, including Sumatran rhinoceroses, elephants, orangutans, and tigers. Bird-watchers can explore a huge network of trails, looking for any of 320 bird species, and the park abounds with reptiles (196 species) and armies of insects and spiders.

The Kerinci Seblat National Park is even larger than Gunung Leuser, with an equally rich variety of wildlife. It is of vital importance to Sumatra's human population because its dense forests act as a sponge, safeguarding supplies of fresh water for many towns and cities. The park is home to two of the world's rarest birds, the Sumatran scops owl and the breathtakingly beautiful Schneider's pitta.

Ujung Kulon National Park in Java is home to one of the last populations of the Javan rhinoceros, along with large herds of bantengs and many large rusas. The brilliant blue-and-purple Javan kingfisher, one of the largest kingfishers in the world and found only on Java, perches there on riverside trees.

The Javan kingfisher is one of the world's largest kingfishers. It lives only in Java.

Check these out:

- Biodiversity
- Deer
- Deforestation
- Endangered Species
- Logging
- Monkey
- National Park
- Orangutan
- Primate
- Rhinoceros

Insect

Insects are small animals with bodies divided into three parts or segments: a head, which bears the eyes and antennae (feelers); a middle section, called the thorax, which bears three pairs of legs and usually one or two pairs of wings; and an abdomen, which contains the sexual organs and sometimes stingers or egg-laying organs.

Insects are invertebrates: they have no internal bones. Instead they have an exoskeleton, a layer of a very hard substance called chitin (KIE-tehn) on the outside of their bodies. Each of its segments has its own chitin armor, with thinner armor between the segments. The animal can bend at the joins between head and thorax and between thorax and abdomen.

At the Heart of the Food Web

Insects absorb heat from their surroundings to keep warm, so the rain forest is a perfect place for them— warm all year round, even at night. Their small size makes them ideal prey for many other animals, but the rain forest provides lots of refuges: dense layers of green leaves, cracks in bark, hollows under tree roots, and dead leaves on the forest floor.

There is abundant food for insects everywhere: leaves, flowers, nectar, pollen, fungi (FUN-jie), dead and rotting plants and animals, other insects, the living bodies of larger animals, and even tiny water creatures in the forest pools and in the water that collects among the leaves of plants such as bromeliads (broe-MEE-lee-ads). With no marked seasons, plants grow year-round in the rain forest. Members of the same plant species may flower and fruit all year, so insects

KEY FACTS

● **About 1 million species of insects are known, but there may be some 9 million species still to be discovered.**

● **One acre of tropical soil can contain about 4 million insects (10 million per hectare).**

● **Mosquitoes can beat their wings up to 600 times a second.**

● **A male cicada makes the loudest noise in the insect world: its signals can be heard 1.4 mi. (2.2 km) away.**

● **The male emperor moth can detect the scent of a female moth from 6.8 mi. (11 km) away.**

● **Fleas may spend up to 90 hours at a time mating.**

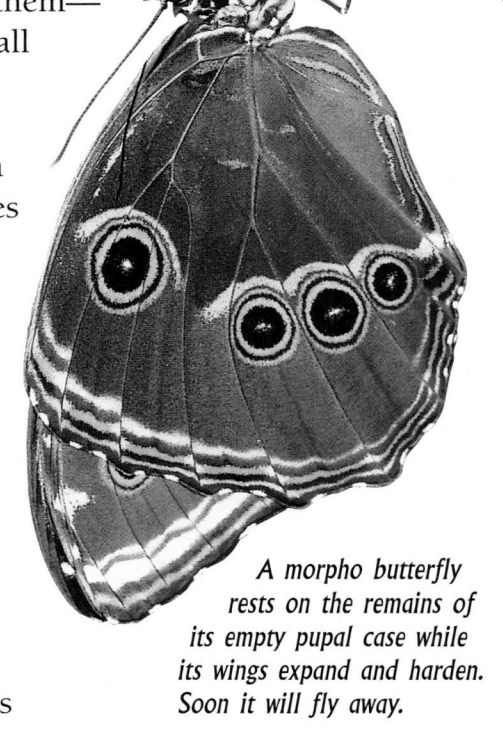

A morpho butterfly rests on the remains of its empty pupal case while its wings expand and harden. Soon it will fly away.

Changing Worlds

Dragonfly and damselfly young, or nymphs (pictured below), live underwater, while their parents live in the air above. When the young are ready for their final molt, they climb up the stems of water plants into the air. Slowly they pull themselves out of their old skeleton, transformed into adult insects with shimmering wings.

time. This is called molting. The new skeleton underneath is soft and stretchy, and the insect pumps itself up with air to stretch it before it hardens.

Before they molt for the last time, the larvae, or young, of butterflies and moths change into a special resting form, the pupa. Protected inside a hard case of skin, the tissues of the larva break down and are rearranged into a completely different-looking animal, the winged adult. This remarkable change is called metamorphosis. Insects such as crickets, grasshoppers, and katydids do not pupate; they start off life as nymphs, miniature versions of their parents.

Designed for Action

The legs and wings of insects come in an astonishing variety of sizes, shapes, and designs. Damselflies and dragonflies have two pairs of wings that appear to beat in different directions as they fly, while the wings of butterflies and moths are linked together and beat as one. The front pair of a beetle's wings form hard cases that protect the delicate underwings, which fold up underneath the cases when at rest.

Worker ants and termites do not usually have wings; only the queens and males do. They use them to make a single mating flight, then shed their wings as they crawl underground to make their nest.

Insect legs may be long and spindly, as on crane flies, or short and stubby, like those of caterpillars. Special elastic-like pads in grasshoppers' knees help them jump. Knobs on their legs make the familiar chirping sound when rubbed together. Bees have bristly pollen baskets on their hind legs, while water beetles use their paddle-shaped legs for swimming.

can afford to specialize in eating just certain kinds of food. It is hardly surprising, then, that there are more varieties of insects in a rain forest than anywhere else on Earth.

The forest relies on insects to pollinate its flowers and break down the remains of dead plants and animals to release nutrients back into the soil for the next generation of forest plants to use. A great variety of other animals rely on the insects themselves for their food.

Growing Up

Most insects lay eggs that hatch into tiny baby insects. In order to grow, an insect has to shed its old skeleton from time to

Exploding Beetles

Insects have some extraordinary ways of defending themselves. Some moths can jam the echolocation of bats, and ladybugs can exude foul-tasting blood from their knee joints when threatened. One of the most amazing defenders is the bombardier beetle, found in rain forests worldwide, that literally fires explosives at its attackers. With a bang it shoots out from the tip of its abdomen a jet of a chemical called benzoquinone at a temperature of 212°F (100°C), which spiders, insects, mice, rats, and birds find extremely unpleasant. The beetle makes the explosive chemical on the spot, mixing less harmful chemicals in a special combustion chamber inside its body.

Helpful Hairs

Insects have many different sense organs. Most insects have hairs scattered over their bodies, especially on their antennae, mouthparts, and legs. These hairs are sensitive to touch and also tell the insect about the pressure it is putting on the ground when walking or on the air when flying, which helps it control its balance and position.

Hairs can also be sensitive to sound. Male mosquitoes can detect females by the pitch of their wing beats, using tufts of hairs on their antennae as ears.

Some hairs can taste and smell. Butterflies taste flowers with their feet before feeding to make sure they are the right kind.

A Colorful World

Insects have color vision, though they may not see colors as humans do. Some can see colors at the ultraviolet end of the spectrum, which humans cannot. Many insects have large compound eyes made up of many tiny individual lenses that form a kind of mosaic picture. This kind of vision is extremely sensitive to movement, which is important for insects when catching prey or avoiding capture. Other insects, such as earwigs, have simple eyes that can only detect light, shadow, and movement.

Insects use color to attract mates and scare off predators. Male butterflies such as heliconiids and nymphalids dance in front of potential mates, showing off their colors and patterns. Certain colors, like patterns of red, orange, or yellow and black, are used as warnings throughout the insect world. Most insects with these colors are poisonous or unpleasant to taste, or they may have poisonous spines or hairs. Once a bird has attacked one such insect and discovered its nasty taste, it will avoid

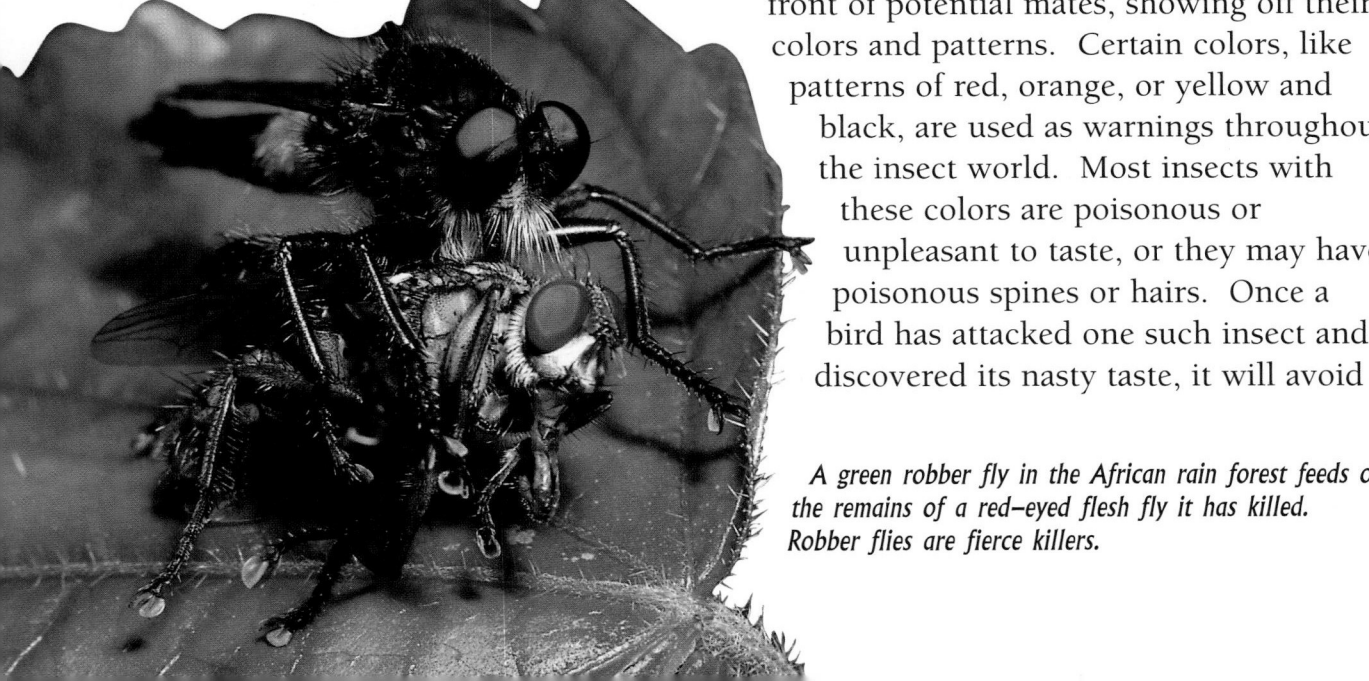

A green robber fly in the African rain forest feeds on the remains of a red-eyed flesh fly it has killed. Robber flies are fierce killers.

The startle display of a Costa Rican eyed silk moth is designed to frighten away attackers. It helps the moth to look like the head of a much larger animal.

all the rest, since they are easy to recognize. Insects get the poisons from the plants they feed on as larvae or caterpillars. For example, the vividly colored heliconiid butterflies of South America feed on passionflowers that contain poisonous chemicals.

Insects can use color to startle a predator, giving the insect a chance to escape. Some moths, such as tropical silk moths and hawkmoths, display brilliantly colored underwings that have markings like large eyes, making predators think they have attacked much larger animals.

Feeding

Many insects are vegetarians, feeding on leaves, flowers, nectar, and plant sap. Aphids' sharp, piercing mouthparts cut through plant stems, and their tubular mouthparts suck up sap. The tubelike mouthparts of butterflies and moths can be rolled up out of the way when not in use. Caterpillars and grasshoppers have sharp, cutting mouthparts for biting and chewing leaves. Some of the toughest mouthparts are those of wood-boring beetles like the harlequin beetle of South America, termites, and wood-boring larvae like those of the South American pantophthalmid fly, the world's largest fly.

Other insects are fierce predators. Robber flies catch other insects on the wing or seize them from perches, while mantises lie in wait for their prey. Army ants from South and Central America and from Africa use their jaws to cut up other insects and even large animals, overpowering their prey by sheer numbers.

Then there are the parasites: lice and ticks that live on the blood of other animals, fly larvae that burrow into their flesh, and a host of others. Some parasites are carried by insects; these are transmitted when the insects bite and may be harmful to humans. For example, mosquitoes carry malaria and sand flies carry leishmaniasis.

Many insects are important decomposers. Fly maggots can reduce a mouse corpse to a skeleton within a few days. Dung beetles, widely distributed in rain forests around the world, bury dung for their larvae to feed on. A host of soil insects helps break down dead leaves and animals.

Check these out:

- Bee and Wasp ● Beetle ● Bug
- Butterfly and Moth ● Decomposer
- Dragonfly ● Fly ● Grasshopper, Cricket, and Katydid ● Invertebrate ● Mantis
- Mosquito ● Parasite

Insectivore

Insectivores are animals that eat insects. Most insectivores also eat other small invertebrates. The word *Insectivora* is used in a more specialized way to describe a particular order of insect-eating mammals that share distinctive skull and teeth features. These "true insectivores" include shrews, moles, and hedgehogs. Of these, only the shrews are common in rain forests.

Insects are not the easiest prey to eat, since they are covered in hard shells, or exoskeletons. Insectivora have sharp, pointed teeth that are all much the same size and shape. These teeth can pierce the shells and shred them. True insectivores do not digest the shells but pass them in their droppings.

A huge range of other animals eat insects, from frogs, toads, and lizards to bats, birds, spiders, fish, and even other insects, such as praying mantises. Some, such as the anteaters, are specialists that feed on particular types of insects; others, like some kinds of wasps, are parasites that lay their eggs inside other insects so that their grubs can feed on them from the inside out.

KEY FACTS

● **Some insect eaters can deal with poisonous or prickly insects. Bee eaters (a kind of bird) remove the stings of their prey before swallowing, while lorises rub hairy caterpillars to remove their irritating hairs before eating them.**

● **Some moths can beat bats at their own game: the moths emit echolocation-blocking sounds that prevent bats from hearing the echo bouncing back from the moths.**

Stalking and Chasing

Insect eaters such as puffbirds, warblers, flycatchers, and toads wait for passing insects to come within reach, then fly or leap out to catch them. Swallows, swifts, and bats chase insects through the air. Bats find their prey by echolocation: they emit high-pitched

This crab spider in New Guinea has captured a cicada (suh–KAE–duh) much larger than itself and is now sucking out the cicada's juices.

sounds and listen for the echoes as they bounce off the insects. Woodpeckers drill into tree bark, searching for grubs. Spiders spin elaborate traps for insects. Chameleons stalk their prey, moving incredibly slowly, one step at a time. Other lizards are more agile, running quickly after their prey.

Tree shrews are small, squirrel-like animals from Southeast Asia that have long narrow snouts for sniffing out insects among the leaves on the forest floor. They will sometimes stretch out their paws and snatch insects that fly past. Armadillos snuffle among the leaves and probe the soil with their snouts and claws, sniffing for grubs. Found from Texas to South America, they have peglike teeth; they feed mainly on ants and termites. Anteaters have no teeth at all and simply suck their prey into their mouth. Anteaters and armadillos have powerful curved claws for tearing into termite and ant nests. Tough skin and bristly hair on their narrow snouts protect them from the bites and stings of angry ants and termites.

Shrews find their prey by listening to the sound of their wings or the scuttling of their feet. Like bats, shrews have acute hearing and can hear high-pitched sounds. Water shrews of tropical Asia hunt in rivers and streams as well as on land. The African otter shrew eats crabs and aquatic insects.

In Australia and New Guinea live small, pouched mammals similar to shrews and hedgehogs—the marsupial mice, possums, rabbit-sized bandicoots, and echidnas (spiny anteaters). They all have uniform pointed teeth like the true insectivores—an example of parallel evolution, where widely separated groups of animals evolve the same characteristics in situations and through lifestyles that are similar.

IN FOCUS

Sticky Tongues

Some insectivores, such as anteaters, armadillos, and pangolins, use long tongues covered in sticky saliva to lap up insects, especially ants and termites. The silky anteater (below) lives in the rain forests of Peru and uses its sticky tongue to fish for ants and termites inside their nests.

Check these out:
- Anteater
- Armadillo
- Bat
- Bird
- Chameleon
- Food Web
- Frog and Toad
- Lizard
- Possum
- Spider

Invertebrate

Rain forest invertebrates range from tiny creatures too small to see with the naked eye to the goliath bird-eating spider of South America, with a leg span of up to 11 inches (28 cm), or the Queen Alexandra's birdwing butterfly of Papua New Guinea, which has a wingspan of 11 inches (28 cm).

Invertebrates are animals without backbones; they have no bony, internal skeleton. Instead they are supported in other ways. Insects, spiders, shrimps, crabs, and lobsters have a hard outer skeleton called an exoskeleton. Snails have a shell into which they can retreat. Worms, slugs, and leeches are completely soft, supported by the pressure of water in their tissues; they have what is called a hydrostatic skeleton.

KEY FACTS

● **Invertebrates make up more than 90 percent of all the animals on Earth. Insects alone, the majority of which are beetles, account for probably 9 million species.**

● **There are about 24,000 species of beetles in all of Canada and the United States, yet a single hectare (2¹/₂ acres) of rain forest may contain over 18,000 species of beetles.**

● **Most invertebrates lay eggs, but a few, including some species of sap-sucking bugs, roundworms, and scorpions, give birth to live young.**

Arthropods

Bugs, beetles, ants, bees, butterflies, spiders, crabs, and millipedes all have one important thing in common: jointed legs. They all belong to a large group (phylum) of invertebrates called the Arthropoda, the joint-legged animals.

RAIN FOREST INVERTEBRATES

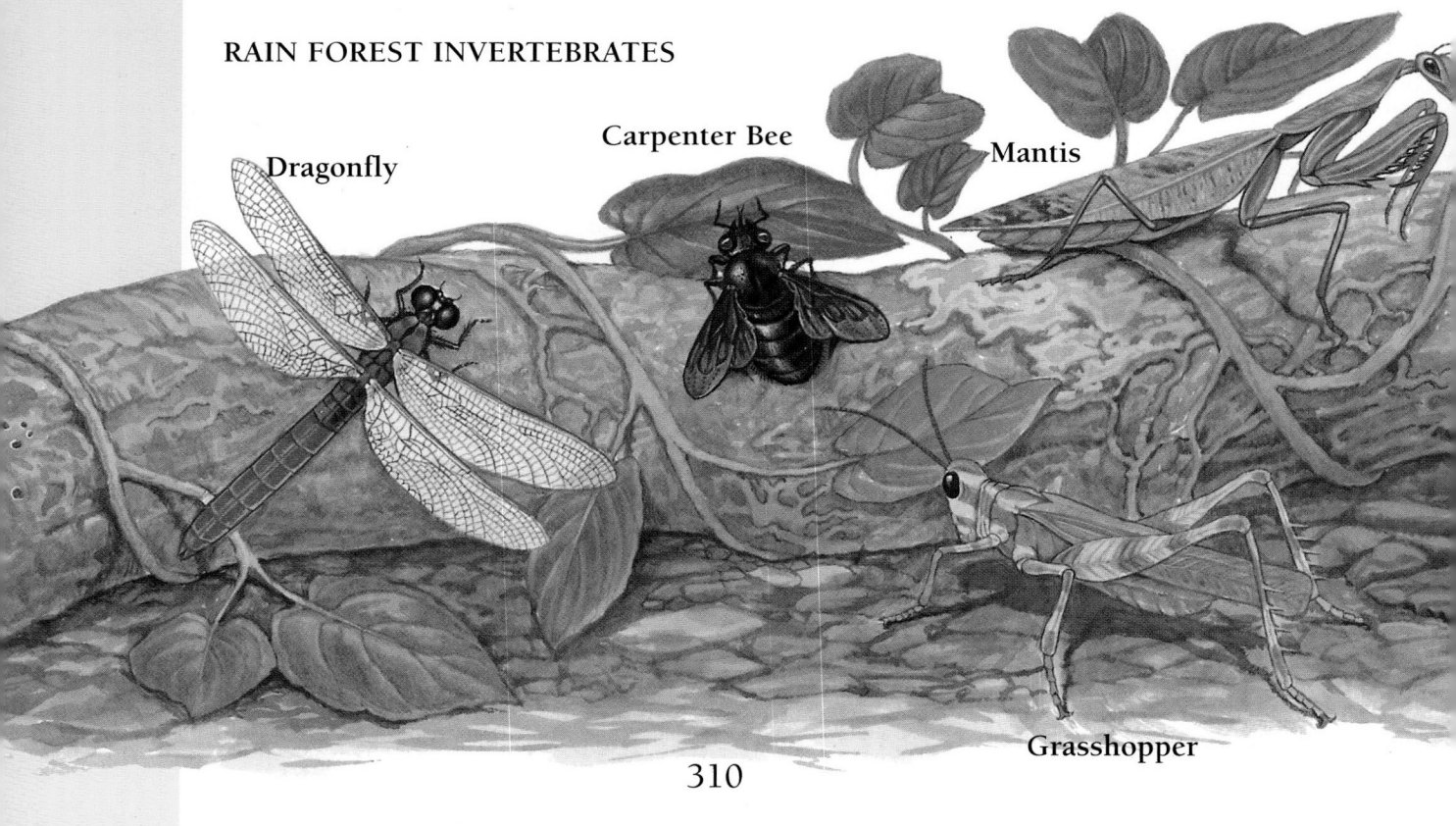

Dragonfly

Carpenter Bee

Mantis

Grasshopper

The hard shell (cuticle) that surrounds their bodies is actually their skeleton. Unlike humans, who have a bony skeleton on the inside that supports all their organs and muscles, arthropods have their skeleton on the outside. Muscles attached to the inside of this skeleton operate the joints. This jointed body plan has allowed arthropods to walk, run, jump, swim, and even fly.

The bodies of arthropods are made up of many sections called segments. Between each segment the cuticle is thinner, so the arthropod can bend its body. Millipedes can wriggle into tiny cracks and crevices, and pill bugs can roll up in a ball to protect their softer underparts.

The hard exoskeleton provides good protection for these small animals. Beetles, for example, fold up their delicate wings under a pair of hard wing cases. Watch a ladybug take off, and you will see it raise its wing cases and spread its wings. The exoskeleton can also make a good

Fatal Encounters

When a praying mantis courts a female, he puts his life in danger. If he does not make a speedy getaway after they have mated, she will attack and eat him. His body will provide a good meal to fuel the development of her fertilized eggs.

weapon. The tough, powerful pincers of crabs are made of cuticle reinforced with a chalky substance.

The hard, sawlike mouthparts of caterpillars and the strong, piercing mouthparts of mosquitoes and plant bugs are also made of hard cuticle. Many arthropods also have jointed feelers (antennae) for touching, smelling, and tasting the world around them. A branching system of tiny tubes (tracheae) carries oxygen from their surroundings into their tissues, and a tubelike heart circulates blood through the body cavity.

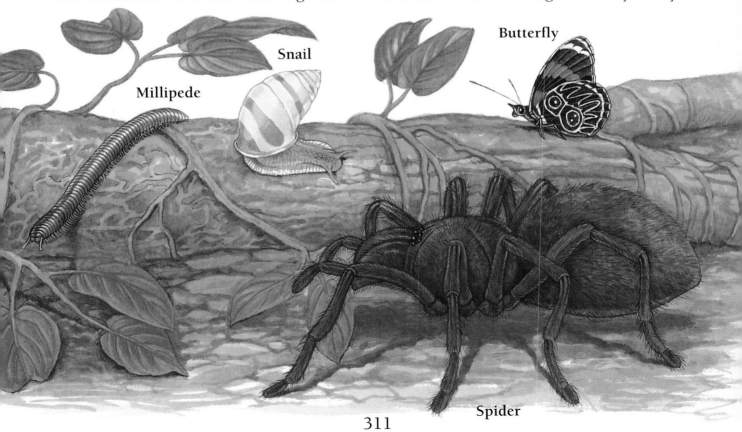

Millipede

Snail

Butterfly

Spider

311

Living Without Legs

Worms, roundworms, slugs, and snails creep along the ground by pushing with their muscles against the fluid inside their bodies. A layer of slime helps them glide over the ground. Earthworms are also helped by small bristles, which they can stick out at will to push against small bumps in the ground. They can also eat their way through the soil, taking in soil through their mouth and passing out the undigestible parts at their tail end, where they form little casts on the ground.

Snails move the same way; their shells only help protect the more delicate parts of their bodies and are not involved in movement. Slugs and snails are mollusks. Their bodies are divided into a kind of head-and-foot section and a hump that contains the digestive organs. In snails and some slugs, the hump secretes a shell that protects the delicate organs within. A snail can also withdraw its entire body into the shell if it is threatened. Snails and slugs have two pairs of soft tentacles, with eyes at the tips of the two upper tentacles.

Mussels, which live in the freshwater rivers of the rain forest, are also mollusks. They do not move. Instead they beat little rows of tentacles to waft water between their open shells, where they filter out tiny water creatures and particles of dead plant and animal remains to eat. Freshwater sponges feed in a similar way, but instead of using tentacles, tiny hairs on the cells lining the pores (holes) in the sponge draw water through its body.

Leeches move quite differently. They have a sucker at each end. Anchored by the rear sucker, they stretch their body forward and fix their front sucker to the ground, leaf, or twig ahead of them, then draw up their rear sucker.

Quite unrelated are the much simpler flatworms,

IN FOCUS

The Velvet Worm

Velvet worms are strange little creatures, like worms with stumpy legs, from just over half an inch to 6 in. (13 to 152 mm) long. Like insects, they have a well-developed brain and a tough outer skin (cuticle). They are found throughout the Tropics under leaves, stones, or logs, in cracks in the soil, and even inside the nests of termites. They feed on small insects, piercing their shells and sucking out their juices. These little animals have probably been around for one billion years. Like worms, they have simple eyes and soft, fluid-filled bodies, so they dry out easily. The moist, humid rain forest is ideal for them.

Robber crabs fight in the coastal rain forest of the Pacific and Indian Oceans. Up to 40 in. (1 m) long and weighing 37 lb. (17 kg), they can crack open coconuts.

flattened wormlike creatures with no nervous systems and no blood circulation. They feed on even tinier animals, moving around by using millions of tiny, beating hairs (cilia) that cover their bodies.

The Breakdown Team

As fast as the forest grows, there are animals trying to consume it. The plants—their leaves, flowers, fruits, sap, wood, and even roots—are all food for some creature.

Chief among these forest vegetarians are the caterpillars. They can do a lot of damage but only for a short time before they metamorphose, turning into butterflies and moths. Grasshoppers and katydids feed mainly on plants, too. Sap-sucking bugs, butterflies, and moths sip nectar from flowers; bees and flower beetles gather pollen; wasps and weevils feast on fruits; and a host of much smaller invertebrates feed on the rotting leftovers

from the feast. Even fungi (FUN-jie) are not safe: they fall prey to fungus flies and fungus beetles.

Wood presents a much greater challenge. Wood eaters need tough, powerful mouthparts for cutting into their food and usually special chambers in their gut where vast populations of bacteria and other microscopic creatures help break down the tough cellulose of the plant cell walls. Termites are notorious in the Tropics for eating wood.

Less obvious are certain moth and fly larvae, including the larvae of some of the largest flies in the world, the pantophthalmid flies of South America. Hatching from eggs laid in wood, these larvae eat their way through the wood, ending up back at the surface again so that

Microbes

Millions of microbes live inside the guts of much larger animals, such as deer and termites. They help to break down tough plant tissues. Other microbes are not so useful. One example is the malaria parasite *Plasmodium*, a single-celled animal that lives in the blood of mosquitoes and other animals, including humans. The dark blobs among these red blood cells are malaria parasites just released from a nearby blood cell.

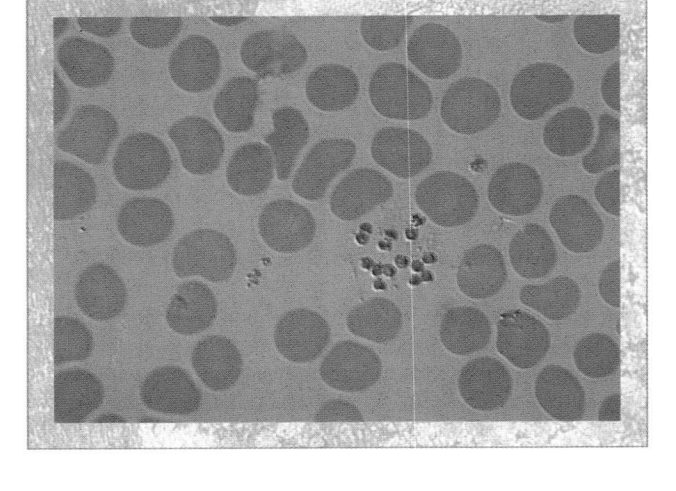

the delicate-winged adults can fly away when they emerge from the pupa. All these grubs provide a feast for predatory beetles and birds such as woodpeckers and for woodwasps, which lay their eggs in the grubs of other insects already inside the wood.

Millipedes and carrion beetles break down dead and decaying plant and animal material on the forest floor. Burying beetles drag corpses into the soil and lay their eggs on them so that their grubs will be able to feed on the flesh. Dung beetles do the same with dung, and skin beetles break down dead skin.

In rain forest rivers and streams, filter-feeding mussels, sponges, freshwater shrimp, and other tiny crustaceans sieve particles of plant and animal material from the water. The mussels and sponges use tiny beating fringes of hairs to filter the water, while the crustaceans have stiffer bristly fringes on their mouthparts and legs. Throughout the rain forest, invertebrates are busy decomposing plant and animal remains, returning valuable nutrients to the soil.

The Invisible Millions

The rain forest has an invisible world with millions of inhabitants, tiny single-celled creatures too small for humans to see without the aid of a microscope. These creatures live on every surface, feeding on microscopic particles of plant and animal remains or on other even smaller creatures such as bacteria. The soil is teeming with them, and so are the mud and water of the pools and lakes in the forest.

These tiny cells are endlessly varied. Amoebas are forever changing shape as they send out lobes of living cell to surround and engulf tiny particles of food. Ciliates whirl around in the tiniest blobs of water, propelled by hundreds of minute beating hairs (cilia), which also draw food particles into their mouth. Other ciliates, shaped like slender trumpets, remain attached to underwater plants and stones and use circlets of hairs at their tips to waft food deep inside.

All these tiny creatures help recycle nutrients in the rain forest. They break down organic particles and release minerals into the water or the soil, where they can be used by plants.

Displays and Deceits

Because some invertebrates are so small, they have many enemies and have evolved a wide range of defenses. The simplest is camouflage: there are mantises that look like flowers, katydids that resemble rotting leaves, and moth pupae that look just like bird droppings. Startle displays can distract a predator just long enough for the prey to make its getaway. Many rain forest hawkmoths flash their wings open to reveal brilliant red-and-orange underwings marked with a pair of large "eyes," giving the impression of a much bigger animal.

Some butterflies are poisonous and advertise this defense with bright red-, orange-, or yellow-and-black patterns. Once a bird has tasted one, it can easily recognize others of the same species and avoid them. Some harmless butterflies mimic these warning colors, gaining the same protection as the distasteful original. *Phyciodes philyra*, which lives in the rain forest of Trinidad, is a mimic that resembles the poisonous Isabella tiger butterfly.

A shield bug, or parent bug, stands guard over her nymphs in the rain forests of New Guinea. Such insects show a high level of parental care.

Some caterpillars swell up and hiss like little snakes. Some ants squirt acid at their attackers, bees and wasps use stings, earwigs and centipedes have nasty bites, spiders and some caterpillars have loose hairs with little barbs that catch in the skin and irritate. Pill bugs roll up, hiding their soft underparts, while velvet worms have one of the strangest defenses of all—they squirt a fast-hardening slime to trap enemies and prey alike.

Mother Love
Few invertebrates take any interest in their offspring. There are some exceptions: centipedes will curl around their eggs until they hatch, licking them occasionally to keep them free from molds and bacteria. Parent bugs or shield bugs, such as the *Cocoteris* from New Guinea, guard their eggs and sometimes also their young for some time, defending them against other insects that might want to eat them. Nursery web spiders from Australia spin special nursery webs in which to keep their young. Others carry them around on their backs once they hatch. In the rain forest, babies the size of large house spiders are carried around by even larger parents.

Without invertebrates, the rain forest as we know it would not exist. A vital link in the food chain, invertebrates provide food for many of the forest's meat eaters and their young. They pollinate flowers and decompose dead organic material, playing a vital role in recycling nutrients.

Check these out:
●Bug ●Butterfly and Moth ●Camouflage ●Crustacean ●Grasshopper, Cricket, and Katydid ●Insect ●Leech ●Mantis ●Mosquito ●Spider ●Termite ●Worm

Jaguar

The jaguar is the only big cat in the Tropics of the Americas. About 6 feet (2 m) from the tip of its nose to the base of its tail—with an extra 2 feet (60 cm) of tail—the jaguar is larger than the leopard, with a broader head and more powerful jaws. It can weigh up to 245 pounds (110 kg). Jaguars live in an area ranging from the southwestern United States to southern Argentina. There are eight subspecies of jaguar; some of them are now very rare.

Jaguars live in dense forests or in swamps close to water. Although they can climb well, they usually hunt on the ground, killing their prey with their powerful paws. They feed on forest mammals, including peccaries (wild pigs), deer, monkeys, tapirs, sloths, agoutis, and capybaras. They also eat birds and small rodents, as well as water creatures such as caimans, frogs, and turtles and their eggs. Jaguars do not dislike water: they often jump in to bathe and even to catch fish.

Raising Young

Jaguars are solitary except during the breeding season. They occupy territories up to 200 square miles (500 km^2), depending on how much food is available. About 100 days after mating, two to four young are born, weighing 1½ to 2 pounds (700 to 900 g). Blind at birth, the cubs open their eyes after 13 days. They are raised by their mother and remain with her for two years, becoming sexually mature at three years old. Jaguars do not roar like most other big cats but utter only growls, grunts, or snarls, though the males mew when they are courting females.

Jaguars in Danger

Jaguars are endangered throughout their range. The largest remaining population is in the rain forests of the Amazon region. The main reasons for their rarity is loss of their habitat and hunting by farmers and ranchers, who accuse them of killing horses and cattle, though this has rarely been proved. Jaguars have been known to live for 22 years in captivity.

Jaguars spend long periods during the day resting in the cooler air above the forest floor.

Check these out:
- Amazonia
- Carnivore
- Cat
- Ecosystem
- Endangered Species
- Food Web
- Mammal

Kaluli People

The Kaluli (KAH-loo-lee) are the largest of four groups of rain forest peoples living in the Southern Highlands Province of Papua New Guinea. The groups together call themselves the Bosavi (BOE-sah-vee). A total of about 2,000 members live in longhouse communities about an hour's walk apart on ridges in the forested mountains. For the last 70 years, they have been moving gradually through the forest in search of better land and to try to escape disease.

Killing the Kaluli

The illnesses started when Europeans first visited the Kaluli in the mid-1930s. The travelers brought with them useful steel axes, knives, and mirrors, but they also carried measles and influenza,

KEY FACTS

● **Kaluli individuals share all the work of the community and also help nearby clan members with their work.**

● **Kaluli songs imitate the sound of wild forest birds.**

● **A Kaluli longhouse may be 60 ft. (18 m) long.**

A view of the Southern Highland region of Papua New Guinea where the Kaluli and other Papuan peoples live.

which eventually killed one-quarter of the Kaluli people. Influenza is still a serious problem for them, in spite of attempts to control it by public health programs, and many children die of it every year. As a result, the Kaluli population is falling slowly but steadily.

Kaluli Life

The Kaluli live by cultivating small garden plots in forest clearings, using each clearing for about three years until the ground is exhausted. Their plots provide bananas, breadfruit, sugarcane, sweet potatoes, and green vegetables. Their staple food is sago (SAE-goe), a starchy paste they extract from wild palms that grow beside streams. In addition they hunt small prey such as lizards and rodents, as well as fish and crayfish from streams. The Kaluli also raise pigs.

The longhouse is the center of the village, standing in a large clearing where the plots are laid out. It may be 30 by 60 feet (9 by 18 m), with porches at the ends. The entire longhouse may sit on poles as high as 12 feet (3.5 m) off the ground. The pigs live underneath. They become excited and noisy at the approach of strangers, acting like watchdogs for the community.

Everyone lives in the longhouse. A community consists of several families with their older relations, about 60 people in all. The fathers sleep on raised platforms in a hall in the middle of the house, while the old men and young boys sleep in a passage along one side, and the women and children on the other, along with piglets too small to be released under the house. Beside each man's sleeping platform is a firebox, where meat is cured, and a pile of firewood. Other possessions

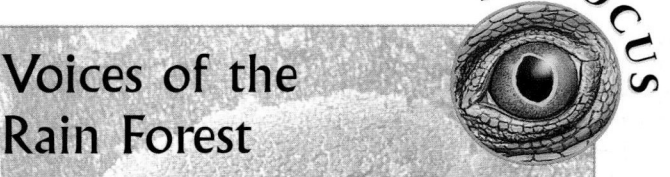

Voices of the Rain Forest

The Kaluli have become famous for their singing, which includes the sounds of forest birds. Many of the birds' calls sound sad, and Kaluli songs are often laments for the loss of friends or relations, expressed in imitations of birdsong. The Kaluli people use birds as a clock and a calendar. Bird calls wake them in the morning, and afternoon calls tell the people when it is time to gather for a meal. Planting and harvesting are started when particular birds are heard singing in the forest.

hang on strings from the rafters to keep them away from rats.

A Life on the Move

Scattered around the clearing stand smaller houses where families live while they are working on their plots, sometimes for two or three weeks at a time. When they can leave their own plots for a while, a family might travel to another village built by people of the same clan to help with the plots there, or they might travel to hunt or trade with villages farther away. This means that the whole community is rarely living in the longhouse at the same time so it is usually not crowded. However, all members of the community plant their plots together, they all share in building the longhouse, and all who are not away working or traveling hunt and fish, cook, and sing together.

Check these out:
● Disease ● Homes in the Rain Forest
● People of the Rain Forest

Kayapo People

The Kayapo (ka-EE-poe) are a native people of the tropical rain forest of the Amazon River basin in South America. They live in central Brazil; their traditional lands lie near the Xingu River, covering a vast area between the Araguaia and the Tapajós Rivers. Some Kayapo people are among the many different groups that have been relocated to Xingu National Park in the southern part of the region.

The Kayapo consist of many different groups with individual names, such as the Mekranoti (MEK-ruh-not-ee). Most Kayapo villages are located near the Xingu

KEY FACTS

● **Today Native Americans constitute only about 0.2 percent of the Brazilian population.**

● **The Kayapo peoples of central Brazil face serious conflicts as gold miners invade their land.**

● **Kayapo protests led the World Bank to withdraw funding for dams that would have flooded their land.**

River, but other Kayapo groups are widely scattered throughout their large territory. They are both hunter-gatherers and farmers, although they depend more on what they gather from the forest than on the crops they grow there.

Some Kayapo groups avoided friendly contact with outsiders until quite recently. The Mekranoti, for example, were not contacted until 1953. Since that time, this group has allowed anthropologists to live with them and learn the Kayapo language, as have other Kayapo groups. The Kayapo have, in turn, learned Portuguese, the national language of Brazil.

The Kayapo's chief, Raoni, in ceremonial dress. Raoni has become renowned internationally for leading the fight to assert Kayapo rights over their land.

319

Meaningful Names

In the Kayapo language, the names of plants and animals can give shades of meaning to other words and phrases. The names of people are also formed this way: special words are added to the names of objects in the Kayapo environment. Naming ceremonies are important events.

Struggle for Survival

The Kayapo face serious problems from the Brazilian government's decision to try to exploit the rain forests for money. Road building has opened Kayapo land to gold seekers, ranchers, and loggers. Massive hydroelectric dam projects threaten to turn their river valleys into lakes.

The Kayapo are notorious in Brazilian history for their fierce resistance to the invasion of their lands by the rubber industry in the 19th century. More recently, they have been among the most skillful tribes in the political arena. In 1989 hundreds of Kayapo organized a protest at Altimira, Brazil, that persuaded the World Bank to withdraw funding for a series of dams that would have flooded Kayapo land. The Kayapo chief, Raoni, became an international leader in the struggle of Amazonian peoples for survival.

Like all Brazilian Indians, the Kayapo have suffered terrible population losses due to European diseases. Smallpox, measles, and even influenza have wiped out entire villages.

Kayapo Life

In Kayapo villages large family homes circle a clearing. In the center stands the men's hut, where the heads of each household discuss the problems of the village and plan ceremonies. The group decides as a whole for the village; the chief does not have the authority to give orders.

The Kayapo have no formal wedding ceremony. A man and woman wishing to be married simply place their hammocks next to each other.

This traditional Kayapo village is being built in the Xingu region of the Brazilian rain forest.

Check these out:
● Disease ● Homes in the Rain Forest
● People of the Rain Forest ● Resettlement

Kuna People

The Kuna (koo-NAH), also *Cuna*, are a native people of the tropical rain forest of Central America. They live along the Caribbean coast of Panama and on the San Blas islands near the coast. About 30,000 Kunas live in more than 60 villages throughout the islands. Kunas also live on a reservation in the rain forest along the coast.

The Kuna had developed a large, highly organized society when the Spanish began colonizing Panama five centuries ago. Their skilled artisans made jewelry and worked with metal and ceramics. Sustainable slash-and-burn farming in the rain forest provided a strong base in agriculture, supplemented by hunting and fishing. Their ancient government consisted of three strong chiefs ruling together.

KEY FACTS

● The Kuna are one of the few indigenous peoples in the world who own their land and who govern themselves.

● At Kuna gatherings, the village chief sings to the people. The songs or chants give advice to his people on daily issues.

● Kuna women are famous for their molas, hand-stitched cloths.

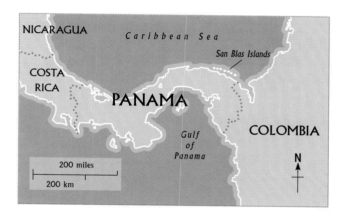

Over the centuries many Kuna moved to the San Blas islands; their isolation from the mainland allowed them to practice their old ways, free of Spanish

The Kuna villages on the San Blas islands are now a popular destination for tourists, providing the Kuna with income from a thriving tourist industry.

interference. It also gave them some protection from the diseases that swept the mainland. The Kuna emerged from the Spanish colonial era with much of their culture intact.

In 1939 Panama signed a treaty with the Kuna, officially recognizing their land reserve. In 1945 the Kuna adopted a constitution based on their ancient system of three chiefs and formalized their status as an independent part of Panama.

Today only Kuna can own land on the Kuna reserve. Everyone there, including Panamanians, are subject to Kuna laws and customs. The Kuna are one of the few native peoples in the world to win these rights.

A Kuna Village

Each Kuna village governs itself in meetings called gatherings, where the men conduct village business. In other kinds of gatherings, all the villagers participate. At these events the village chief sings to the people. The songs or chants give advice to the villagers on issues of daily life.

Kuna Wildlands Project

The Kuna have been widely recognized for setting aside a large portion of their rain forest as a forest preserve, called the Kuna Wildlands Project. In the core area of the preserve, only scientific research is allowed. Other areas of the preserve include a portion for agriculture and a portion for cultural activities.

Kuna women are famous for their needlework. They create multilayered, hand-stitched cloth called molas. The molas are square panels with intricate designs in bright colors that are sewn to the front and back of clothing. Selling molas provides income for many Kuna women.

Rain forest crops, including sugarcane, rice, coconuts, and fruit, continue to be important for the Kuna. The plantain, a fruit similar to bananas, is the largest crop. The Kuna have many different ways of preparing plantains as both a food and a beverage. Today Kuna coconut crops are said to be the best in the world.

The clear water and coral reefs of their islands support an important tourist industry. However, many Kuna travel by boat each day to work on Panama's mainland.

Kuna needlework patterns, known as molas, use bright colors and shapes. This design is known as stingray.

Check these out:

● People of the Rain Forest

Leaf

Leaves are often called the factories of the plant world because almost all of a plant's food is made in its leaves. The food-making process is called photosynthesis; by combining water and carbon dioxide, the plant produces a simple sugar called glucose. The energy needed for the process comes from sunlight, which is absorbed by the leaves' green or purple coloring, called chlorophyll. Most chlorophyll is packed into the upper layers of the leaf, where it can absorb the greatest amount of sunlight. The upper surface therefore tends to be much darker than the lower surface. Everything that the plant needs to survive can be made from the glucose and various minerals obtained from the soil.

Tough-walled veins support the leaf blade and carry the essential water to it. They also carry the glucose away, through the leafstalk, to other parts of the plant. The leaf's bottom surface is dotted with microscopic pores called stomata, through which carbon dioxide from the air enters the leaf. Water vapor also escapes through the pores, and the water evaporating from there pulls more water up from the roots. This entire process is called transpiration.

A drop of water falling from the tip of a rain forest leaf. Many rain forest leaves have long, slender drip tips that allow rainwater to drain away quickly.

Rain Forest Leaves

The leaves of many rain forest trees look alike because they are all adapted to cope with similar conditions. They are generally small or medium-sized and quite tough, enabling them to withstand the heavy rain. Most have smooth edges and a shiny upper surface. Many also have long, pointed tips called drip tips, which are especially common in the wettest parts of the forest. All these features help the water run off quickly.

Rain forest trees are mostly evergreens, which means they have leaves throughout the year. However, that does not mean that the leaves last forever. Individual leaves may survive for only a year or two. While many deciduous trees in the temperate regions become brilliantly colored when their leaves are about to fall, rain forest trees tend to be most colorful when their leaves are

Dangerous Leaves

The rain forests of Southeast Asia and northern Australia contain some particularly unpleasant trees. Related to stinging nettles, they are called stinging trees, and touching their leaves can cause severe pain. The largest species is the giant stinging tree (shown here) from tropical Queensland, which reaches heights of about 130 ft. (40 m). *Dendrocnide moroides*, which grows in the same area, is a small shrub but presents an even greater danger to animals because its leaves usually grow up to 6 ft. (2 m), within easy reach of many animals. Hollow glassy hairs cover the large heart-shaped leaves of both species. When the leaves are touched, the tips of the hairs break off and the jagged edges pierce the skin, injecting a strong poison. However, many insects, including some caterpillars and stick insects, are unaffected by the poisons; they can munch their way through the leaves unharmed, while benefiting from the protection from other predators the stinging leaves afford.

opening. The young leaves are often red or orange, and are produced in two or three bursts each year. At that time, whole trees may change color and look as if they are in flower.

Because the dense canopy cuts off most of the light, the rain forest floor is extremely dim. Plants growing near the ground often overcome this problem by having extra-large leaves that trap as much light as possible. Low-growing leaves often contain dark pigments, especially deep reds or purples, because dark colors absorb light better than pale colors.

Under Attack

Huge numbers of caterpillars and other insects feed on rain forest leaves. Some monkeys exist mainly on leaves, and the sloths of South America eat nothing else; however, very few birds eat them. The leaves of many rain forest trees are protected by bitter-tasting substances, and these are rejected by most animals.

Check these out:
● Herbivore ● Photosynthesis ● Plant
● Shade Toleration ● Tree

Leech

Small wormlike animals, most leeches feed on the blood of other animals, called hosts. They have a large sucker at the tail end for anchoring themselves to their host or to leaves or twigs. The front end also has a sucker surrounding the mouth.

Other leeches feed on decaying plant and animal matter or prey on smaller animals such as snails, worms, and insect larvae. Some leeches live on the forest floor.

A leech moves by sticking its rear sucker to a leaf surface, then stretching forward and sticking its front sucker down some distance away. As it does this, its body becomes long and thin. It then releases the rear sucker and pulls the rest of its body up to the front one.

There are about 300 different kinds of leeches; some grow to over 8 inches (20 cm) long. Leeches are hermaphrodites—each animal is both male and female. When they mate, a pair of leeches fertilize each other's eggs.

Anchored by its rear sucker, a leech explores its surroundings in search of a likely meal.

Painless Parasites

Many leeches live in streams and lakes, where some feed on fish. Other animals may suck the leeches into their mouths or noses while drinking. Leeches are most common in the rain forests of Asia. There, they sometimes kill domestic animals by invading their lungs and blocking the breathing passages.

Leeches have three jaws with sharp teeth that make a Y-shaped cut in the flesh of their host. They cover the wound with saliva, which contains chemicals that act like an anesthetic, so the host feels no pain. Other chemicals in the saliva prevent the blood from clotting and widen the blood vessels so that the blood flows faster. Leeches can store blood or other food for several months in a special pouch in their gut.

For humans walking through the rain forest, the first hint of a leech may be the trickle of blood from an ankle. Leech bites are not harmful, but people must make sure the wounds do not get infected.

Check these out: ● **Invertebrate** ● **Locomotion** ● **Parasite** ● **Worm**

Lemur

Lemurs (LEE-muhrs) are primates that live in the forests of Madagascar and nearby islands. There are about 20 different species. The smallest, the mouse lemurs, are about the size of a mouse, while the indri is almost as big as a chimpanzee. Unlike other primates, such as monkeys with their flatter faces, lemurs have pointed, foxlike snouts with long sensitive whiskers, moist black noses, and furry faces. Most have long furry tails, but a few, such as the indri, have almost no tails at all. The smaller lemurs are nocturnal, but the larger species come out to feed in the daytime.

KEY FACTS

● Most lemur species are seriously endangered and may well become extinct before the end of the century.

● The word *lemur* means "ghost." The tiny faces peering between the branches and the spooky cries of some lemurs make them seem like wild spirits.

● Most lemurs have four lower front teeth that point forward, forming a tooth comb for grooming, eating vegetation, and in some species for scraping gum out of crevices in the bark of trees.

● The indri, a large black-and-white lemur, can leap a distance of 30 ft. (9 m) between trees.

Out of Africa

The island of Madagascar became cut off from mainland Africa about 50 million years ago, when the ancestors of both monkeys and lemurs were already on the island. While monkeys, chimpanzees, gorillas, and orangutans

were evolving on mainland Africa and Asia, the lemurs evolved quite separately on their island home, forming very different animals. At one time there were as many as 40 different kinds of lemurs, each adapted to a different forest habitat and to different foods. Some were quite unlike modern lemurs: there were lemurs that swung through the trees by their arms; lemurs that foraged on the ground like pigs; and lemurs as large as giant koalas, with skulls over 1 foot (30 cm) long.

The female black lemur is not black at all, but a glorious chestnut brown. The male is jet black.

More than half these species disappeared about 1,300 years ago when humans arrived. They were hunted for food, their habitat was destroyed by fire or felled for farming, and they had to compete for food and space with the settlers' cattle and goats. Forest once covered Madagascar, but today only a few isolated patches remain. Even these are at risk of being cleared for farming as the human population grows. However, local people are beginning to realize the value of lemurs in attracting eco-tourists, people interested in seeing the natural world without harming it.

Leaping Lemurs

Lemurs live in trees and are great climbers. Most walk along branches on all fours, but some leap from branch to branch and tree to tree, using their long tail to help them balance. Lemurs usually come to the ground only where the trees are far apart. The sifaka and the indri will hop rapidly across the ground on their hind legs, holding their arms above their head.

Family Life

A few lemurs, such as the sportive lemur, live alone, but most live in small family groups. Usually only one young is born at a time, after a three- to five-month pregnancy, but some of the smaller lemurs have two or three young at once. The baby clings to its mother's belly until it is big enough to ride on her back.

Male and female lemurs are about the same size, but in some species they are different colors. For instance male black lemurs are jet black, while females are reddish or golden brown with striking white ear tufts. Other lemurs range from black and gray to brown, gold, and even pure white.

The Gentle Lemur

Most lemurs are vegetarians, eating leaves, fruits, and flowers. Gentle lemurs are specialists: they feed only on bamboo stems and reeds. They pull shoots through a special gap between their teeth to strip off the tough outer layers.

IN FOCUS

Check these out:
- Endangered Species ● Madagascar
- Mammal ● Monkey ● Primate

Lichen

Lichens (LIE-kuhns) are hardy plantlike organisms, each of which consists of a fungus in a close partnership with an alga. The latter is a tiny green plantlike organism able to make its own food by photosynthesis. Although the fungus forms the bulk of the lichen, with the tiny algae bound up inside, it cannot exist by itself. It needs its algal partner to provide it with food. Lichens were once treated as a distinct group of plants, but most biologists now regard them as special kinds of fungi (FUN-jie) that cannot exist by themselves. However, the various kinds of algae that partner with the fungi can live by themselves.

KEY FACTS

● **A lichen consists of a fungus and an alga growing together in a close partnership.**

● **Lichens are very hardy, but the one thing they cannot tolerate is air pollution. Many lichens in an area can indicate that the air is quite clean.**

Although fungi or mushrooms are generally soft, delicate organisms, most lichens are very tough and extremely hardy. They can survive in some of the hottest and driest places on Earth, as well as in some of the coldest places—environments in which it would be quite impossible for fungi or algae to live by themselves. Lichens can grow in sun-scorched deserts and on the rocks and frozen ground around the snow line on high mountains. They grow extremely slowly, in great contrast to the molds and other fungi that can smother a slice of stale bread in a few hours. Most lichens would take many years to cover the same area.

Forest Lichens

Lichens grow as epiphytes on the trees in most temperate woodlands. In regions with plenty of rainfall, they can cover almost every trunk and branch. One might think that rain forests would also be good for lichens, but lichens are actually less common there than in the cooler woodlands. They tend to be swamped by the quicker-growing mosses and ferns and the abundant orchids.

Most rain forest lichens grow high up in

The orange patches on this lichen, found clothing a tree trunk in the African rain forest, contain millions of minute fungus spores.

IN FOCUS

Getting Food

Both partners in a lichen have a role to play in feeding. The fungus usually absorbs water and minerals from the surface on which it is growing and then passes them to the algae. The algae usually form a layer near the outer surface, where they can absorb the sunlight necessary for photosynthesis. The sugar they make is shared with the fungus.

the sunlit zone of the canopy, which is drier than the lower levels and experiences more variation in temperature and humidity. Mosses do not thrive in this environment and so do not smother the lichens. The *Parmelia* species of lichens, which look like crinkled leaves, are among the most common of the treetop lichens.

Forests growing on mountain slopes in the Tropics are often permanently misty. Called cloud forests, they are cooler than the lowland forests, and many lichens grow on the trees there. The slender *Usnea* species often hangs from the branches like huge beards. Some rain forest lichens such as the *Strigula* species even grow on the leaves, although most leaves have shiny surfaces where lichen spores cannot get a good hold.

New Plants from Old

Lichens reproduce in two different ways. Tiny flakes containing pieces from both partners regularly break off from the surface and are carried away by the wind or rain. Those that land in a small pore in bark or rocks can grow into new lichens. The lichens also scatter minute, dustlike spores, which are often produced in brightly colored patches on the lichens' surface. These spores are made only by the fungal partner, and although they can start to grow, they cannot survive for long unless they meet the right kind of alga. Some lichens can live for several hundred years, but only if the air is fairly clean; scientists have discovered that few lichens can tolerate air pollution, making them important indicators of air quality.

Rain forest lichens, such as these growing on a tree trunk in South America, are mostly leaflike. Elsewhere, lichens form thin crusts on bark and rocks.

Check these out:
- **Fungus** ● **Photosynthesis** ● **Plant**

329

Light Gap

Rain forest soils are thin, with all the available nutrients close to the surface. Rain forest trees spread wide, shallow roots to better absorb these nutrients. A strong wind can flip the tallest tree over, bringing down with it smaller trees growing nearby. This leaves a large break in the canopy called a light gap. Light gaps are also made by small localized fires and by human activity, when people clear small patches of land for crops or settlements. This is what plants on the ground have been waiting for.

The Race for Light

Some plants are adapted to living in the dim light of the forest floor. Ivies, ferns, and mosses, for example, typically have dark green leaves, able to make use of the small amounts of sunlight that can reach the ground through the canopy. However, the plants that are waiting for the light gap to appear are not specially adapted, except by being able to survive, sometimes for years, in poor conditions.

When a light gap opens up, these plants grow rapidly in dense stands, covering the forest floor so that sometimes it is impossible to walk through them. Soft herbaceous plants, often with long ribbonlike leaves to collect as much light as possible, are the first to appear. Alongside them, creepers push upward, reaching for a tree to climb to lift their leaves into the canopy. Among these are the saplings of forest trees.

WHEN A TREE FALLS

A tree collapses in the forest and allows a shaft of light to penetrate the usually dark interior.

Ferns and tree seedlings are activated by the increased sunlight and begin to sprout.

An agouti (uh–GOO–tee) forages for food in a light gap in Panama. Agoutis feed mainly on fallen fruits.

The first saplings to grow are the smaller, relatively short-lived trees, which form a thick understory that might last for 100 years. Among them, waiting for the short-lived trees to die, are the forest giants, such as teak, mahogany, and kapok trees, which will finally have their turn, beginning a life that will be measured in centuries.

Animals in the Light

Light gaps are important not only to plants; they are also vital to the survival of many insects and the birds and other animals that feed on them. Flowers are scarce in the darkness of the forest floor; only in light gaps can they find enough ultraviolet light to enable them to grow and bloom. Butterflies need flowers for their nectar, and during the breeding season the males of some species defend well-lit patches of flowers to attract females to mate with. Bees and flowerflies also feed at flowers, as well as hummingbirds and other nectar eaters.

In the darkness of the rain forest, light gaps provide welcome living space for a wide variety of animals and plants, and they give the forest a chance to renew itself when the largest and oldest trees come to the end of their life.

IN FOCUS

Feeding Elephants

African forest elephants love to feed on secondary forest vegetation, new growth that springs up in light gaps. Selective logging creates light gaps similar to those that would happen naturally, and the resulting growth of vegetation is actually beneficial to the elephants.

Check these out:
- Dormancy ● Plant ● Shade Toleration

Tree saplings take hold and overtake the ferns. A race begins among the saplings to reach the canopy.

The saplings have grown into forest giants and closed up the light gap.

Lizard

Lizards are four-legged reptiles that live on land. Like all reptiles, they are covered with scaly skin and are cold-blooded. This means they rely on warmth from their surroundings to raise their body temperature so that they can become active. The rain forest is an ideal place for cold-blooded animals because it is warm day and night all year round.

Most lizards have long, tapering tails. Their legs stick out sideways so they waddle and twist as they walk. Using claws on their toes or tiny suction pads, lizards can cling to tree trunks and even vertical leaves; they can easily climb to the tops of the forest trees. Some, such as the worm lizards, prefer to burrow into the forest floor in search of insect grubs.

Only a few lizards, such as the iguanas, feed on plants; most are predators. Some of the large monitors can capture prey as large as deer and may also eat carrion. Other lizards feed mainly on insects or small mammals such as mice. Since there are more insects and other sources of food in the rain forest than in any other habitat, lizards of all shapes and sizes flourish there.

Lizard Vision

Lizards have good color vision, and their bright, alert eyes are far enough forward in the head to allow them to judge distance and speed when catching their prey. Their lower eyelids can be moved to wipe the eyes. The lower lids of some burrowing lizards form transparent "safety glasses" that protect the eyes from soil particles. Since its lower eyelids cannot wipe its eyes, the lizard has to lick them clean with its tongue.

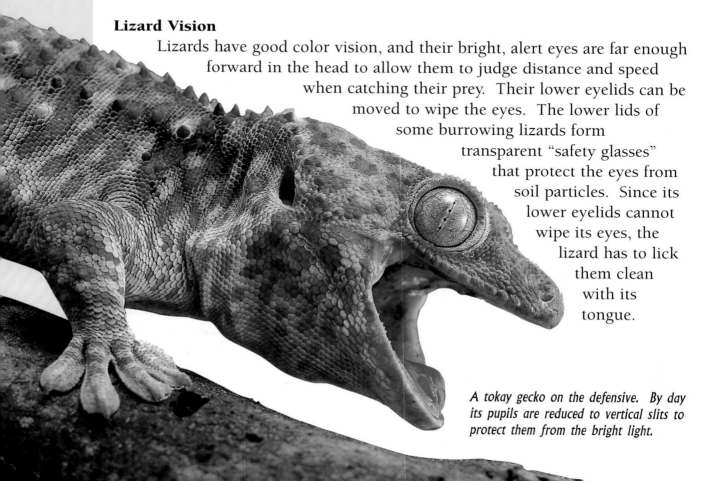

A tokay gecko on the defensive. By day its pupils are reduced to vertical slits to protect them from the bright light.

Chameleons (kuh-MEEL-yuhns) have unique eyes mounted on little turrets. Each eye can move independently of the other, so a chameleon can look in two directions at once. This helps it spot prey. Most lizards hunt by day, but some lizards and many geckos come out at night. Their eyes are particularly sensitive to low light levels, and by day the pupil closes to a vertical slit with just a few chinks to let light in.

Lizards also have a third eye, a light-sensitive disk on the top of their head that can detect light and dark. It probably governs the lizard's internal biological clock, which controls the animal's behavior during day and night.

Other Senses

Lizards have reasonably good hearing through an ear opening toward the back of their head. A few burrowing lizards have no external ear opening. Instead these lizards hear through the vibration of bones in their skulls.

Lizards do not make many sounds, though some may hiss when threatened or annoyed. However, geckos, which often come out at night, do use sounds to communicate with each other. The most famous is the barking gecko, or tokay gecko, of Asia, which lives in and around people's houses. During the mating season, the male tokay gecko makes a loud barking sound.

Lizards also use their sense of smell to tell them about food, predators, other lizards' territories, and potential mates. Like snakes, they have extra organs of smell, the Jacobson's organs, in special pits in the roof of the mouth. Lizards that rely heavily on smell continually flick their forked tongue to waft air into these organs.

Real Dragons

Komodo dragons live on the tropical Komodo Island and nearby islands in Indonesia. Up to 12 ft. (3.5 m) long, the Komodo dragon is powerful enough to attack and kill a human, but it feeds mainly on carrion. Deadly bacteria that live in the Komodo dragon's saliva will infect bite wounds, eventually killing its victims. This provides the Komodo with a meal days after it has bitten its prey. Baby Komodo dragons live in trees, but the fierce adults, which have few enemies, live on the ground.

Hunting for Food

Most lizards feed on insects and small mammals; their teeth are topped with three points for grabbing, holding, and crunching their prey. Lizards do not chew their food but swallow it whole or in chunks. The marine skink of the South Pacific has blunt back teeth similar to human molars for crushing the shells of crabs. The teeth of the Komodo dragon have sawlike edges for cutting into the flesh of large animals such as deer.

While the chameleons of Africa stalk their prey extremely slowly, many lizards simply stand still and wait for insects to fly or scuttle within reach. Some will dig up the eggs of turtles and other animals. A few will actively chase their prey.

The water monitors of India and the Pacific Ocean actually catch fish. Holding their legs close to their body, they swim underwater, swinging their tails from side to side to propel themselves. Sometimes they submerge to escape enemies. Some lizards can stay underwater for a whole hour.

Careless Parents

In tropical regions many lizards breed all year round. Most lizards lay their leathery-shelled eggs where predators are not likely to discover them—under the bark of trees, in cracks or holes in tree trunks, under tree roots or dead leaves, or in caves. Then they abandon them to their fate. Geckos and green iguanas (ih-GWAH-nuhs) may use communal nesting sites, where several females lay their eggs. Small species of lizards lay only one or two eggs, but large lizards such as iguanas may lay over 50 eggs at a time.

A few skink mothers stay with their eggs until they hatch, turning them over from time to time. Some lizard mothers have no choice: the eggs remain inside their bodies until they hatch, so they "give birth" to live young. Many tropical skinks produce live young. The young of the Brazilian skink are actually attached to their mother's womb by a placenta, just as in humans.

Baby lizards have a special egg tooth on their snout, which they use to break through the eggshell when they hatch. This tooth falls off soon afterward.

Showing Off

Lizard courtship displays are some of the most interesting in the animal world. Many lizards try to impress their mates by showing off colorful throat pouches, crests, or other patches of color. Some, such as the iguanas and their relatives, have crests along their heads and backs that look fearsome when erect. Others swell their brilliantly colored throat pouches to a great size. Jerky head bobbing draws attention to the throat pouches and is also good for displaying crests. Elaborate and energetic push-ups or tail waving will reveal a colorful belly. Monitor lizards go one step further and engage in wrestling matches while standing on their hind legs.

This Costa Rican anole is shedding its skin. The new skin will be loose and soft for a time.

Legless Lizards

For lizards that burrow in the soil, tunnel through dense vegetation, or live in narrow cracks in rocks, legs can be a nuisance. In the course of evolution, some lizards have "lost" their legs. The strange worm lizards, found in tropical and subtropical parts of the West Indies, the Americas, Africa, and Southwest Asia, have powerful heads, which they use like corkscrews to bore into the soil. With its thick, strong skull, the lizard rams its head into the soil, then twists its body around and around. Worm lizards have no legs, no external ears, and only minute traces of eyes.

Many male lizards also display to intimidate other males and defend a territory. These threat displays may involve showing off a red or orange mouth lining. Holding a territory makes sure the owner will have enough food around to support a family and gives him access to all the females in the area. The downside to all this displaying is that it also attracts the attention of predators.

Keeping Safe

Most lizards are small enough to make a tasty morsel for larger animals, but they have many ways of keeping safe. Most can run quickly, changing direction frequently until they can squeeze into a crack or under a bush. The basilisk, a lizard of Central and South America, runs so fast that it can sprint across water on its hind legs, not staying anywhere long enough to sink. A few lizards, such as iguanas, will leap into a stream or pond and stay underwater until the danger has passed.

Many lizards rely on camouflage to hide from their enemies. Some geckos can match the colors and patterns of their background, even mimicking the surface texture of bark. Many anoles (uh-NOE-lees) are as bright green as the leaves they live on. The chameleon is not the only lizard that can change color: many lizards can turn darker or lighter according to the time of day or the color of the background.

Skinks and geckos have a surprise for their attackers—they can shed the end of their tail at will along a special line of weakness simply by contracting certain muscles. The shed tail twitches and wriggles, distracting the predator's attention from the fleeing lizard. The lizards can grow a new, though weaker, tail—a small price to pay for their escape. Other lizards simply pretend to be dead. Monitors may puff themselves up to look even fiercer than they already do, while blue-tongued skinks stick out their huge, bright blue tongue to startle and frighten attackers.

Check these out:

- Chameleon   ● Communication   ● Gecko
- Iguana   ● Insectivore   ● Reptile

Locomotion is the way animals move. The rain forest presents many challenges for animals—they may need to climb trees, balance on or hang from branches, move from tree to tree, cross the forest floor, or even ford rain forest streams. Animals with skills such as tree climbing can reach food that other animals cannot. Animals that can move from tree to tree without coming down to the ground may be able to avoid certain predators such as tigers and jaguars.

KEY FACTS

● **The basilisk lizard can run on water. It rears up on its hind legs and runs over the water so fast that it does not have time to sink.**

● **Tree frogs have suckers on their toes for clinging to vertical leaves.**

● **Geckos have many tiny ridges on the soles of their feet that can grip the slightest unevenness in a surface. They can even cling to vertical windowpanes.**

● **A flea can jump 130 times its own height.**

Walking and Sliding

Lizards and alligators move diagonally opposite legs at almost the same time, so their bodies twist from side to side as they walk. Their legs stick out sideways from their torso, so the largest of these animals cannot lift their bodies far off the ground. Frogs and toads, if not jumping, also have a similar movement. In contrast the legs of mammals are positioned directly under their body, so they are much more effective for support when walking.

A red-eyed leaf frog assumes a streamlined shape as it soars through the air in a powerful leap.

Mammals move their legs in a different sequence, so they do not wiggle as they walk.

Having no legs may appear to be a disadvantage, but snakes can squeeze through narrow openings in search of prey, and they move very quietly as they approach unsuspecting animals. Snakes, worms, and leeches all manage to move without using legs. As a snake slithers, it throws its body into curves that press back against stones and other objects on the ground. This propels it forward. The scales can also act like little levers. Each has its own set of muscles and can push against the surface of the ground. Worms and leeches have soft, tubelike bodies full of fluid. They use their muscles to squeeze the fluid and make themselves long and thin. Then they relax these muscles and use another set to grow short and fat again. They anchor part of their body to the ground and stretch forward, then anchor the front end and draw the rest of the body up to meet it. Some caterpillars move in a similar way.

The High Life

Jumping calls for powerful hind legs. Frogs and toads have much larger back legs than front legs. When powerful muscles straighten these legs, the feet push down and back against the ground, propelling the frog into the air. The leg bones act like a set of levers, pivoting at the joints. Frogs rely on leaping, perhaps into the nearest pond or stream, to escape from predators.

The ability to climb trees means that an animal can exploit the rich sources of food—leaves, flowers, insects—in the canopy. It can also climb to escape predators that live on the ground, and it can rear its young out of their reach. Many mammals and birds can climb trees, digging their claws into the bark. Some mammals—and a few lizards—use their tail like an extra limb, curling it around a branch or even swinging from it while they try to reach another branch. Birds such as woodpeckers use their tails as supports when they move up and down tree trunks.

For many animals it is safer to move from tree to tree without

---

IN FOCUS

Clinging to Trees

Most birds have three toes directed forward and one backward, rather like a thumb, for grasping twigs. Some, like the woodpeckers, have two toes directed backward. This helps brace the bird on a vertical tree trunk as it looks for food.

---

going down to the ground where predators lurk. Moving from tree to tree requires extra skills. Monkeys and gibbons swing along branches with their arms, their hands forming hooks to grip the branches. Chimpanzees and squirrels walk along branches on all fours, then leap to the next tree.

The sifaka is a great leaper, trailing its long tail as a counterbalance while in the air. Its lightning-quick reactions help it

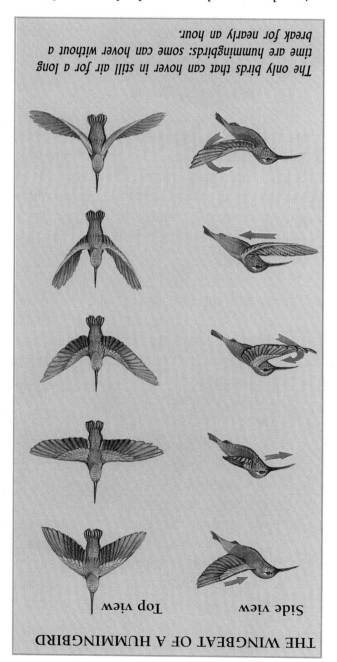

THE WINGBEAT OF A HUMMINGBIRD

Side view   Top view

The only birds that can hover in still air for a long time are hummingbirds: some can hover without a break for nearly an hour.

grab the tree trunk or branches the moment it touches the bark. Some snakes simply fling themselves off a branch, hoping to land on another one.

Getting Airborne

The safest way to travel is to fly. When a bird or insect flies, its wings beat down and back so that they push on the air to generate forward and upward thrust. Wings have a large surface area to push against the air. Both birds and insects rotate their wings as they fly, pushing down and back on the power stroke and slicing almost vertically up through the air on the up stroke. Most insects beat both pairs of wings at the same time, but dragonflies beat them at different times, rotating them as they fly.

Birds fold their wings on the upstroke to reduce the area pushing on the air. Then they spread their feathers out on the downstroke for maximum push. The wing of a bird is a special shape that creates reduced air pressure above the wing as the bird moves forward and increases pressure below it. This creates lift.

A bird's feathers can be spread out, closed, or twisted to help the bird steer, and its legs and tail can be lowered to act as brakes. A thick, dense forest is not a good place for fast flyers, but some hawks manage it. They have short, rounded wings and a long tail for maneuvering through the trees.

Gliding Animals

Some animals have evolved an almost effortless way of moving from tree to tree—they glide through the air. Most of these gliders live in dense tropical forests, where the trees are close together and gliding distances small. The flying squirrels of Central America and the marsupial gliders of Australia have large, furry sheets of skin that stretch out from their bodies to their wrists and ankles. They launch themselves into the air and spread out their arms and legs, gliding down to the next tree trunk.

Some surprising animals glide. The Asian flying lizard has flaps of skin that act like sails and allow it to glide. The flying frog of Central America uses huge webbed feet as parachutes. Flying snakes, of which there are several species in rain forests around the world, flatten their bodies to break their fall.

The Asian flying lizard has long flaps of skin that it can spread between its ribs to help it glide.

Paddling, Rowing, and Diving

In the tropical rain forests, many pools of water never dry up. Some forests are flooded at certain times of year, allowing animals that can swim an escape from the rising water and an easy route to find new food sources.

There are four main ways of moving through water if you are not a fish: paddling, rowing, kicking, or wiggling. Animals that paddle usually have either webbed feet or fins, but water beetles have thick fringes of bristles on their flattened legs that act like little paddles.

Insects such as water boatmen row themselves along with paddle-shaped limbs. Paddlers include many ducks and other waterbirds, otters, and the capybaras of South America.

Some diving birds, such as grebes, fold their wings close to their bodies as they dive, propelling themselves with their feet. Grebes are found throughout the Tropics. Darters and anhingas (also known as snakebirds) use their wings to "fly" underwater.

Frogs and toads swim in a special way called the frog kick. It looks like the human breaststroke. The frog draws its hind legs close to its body, then pushes them back quickly, spreading its huge webbed feet at the same time. It uses its front legs for steering and balancing.

Salamanders and alligators swim quite differently. Like snakes, they flex their bodies from side to side, each curve pushing back and sideways at the same

Flightless Birds

In the rain forests of New Zealand and Australia and on some Pacific islands live birds that cannot fly. Birds that can find plenty of food on the ground do not need to fly, except to escape from predators. Before humans arrived, New Zealand and many oceanic islands had no mammalian predators on the forest floor, and birds such as the flightless kiwi (below) flourished.

time. They also use their webbed feet to help them swim forward.

Some insects, such as water striders and marsh treaders, are so light they can walk on the surface of the water. Brushes of hairs on their feet help spread their weight over a wide area, keeping them from breaking through the water's surface.

Check these out:
● Bird ● Bug ● Canopy ● Fish ● Frog and Toad ● Insect ● Leech ● Lizard ● Mammal ● Monkey ● Reptile ● Snake

Logging

Rain forest trees grow very slowly and can be huge. Their long, straight trunks, with the fine grain produced by slow growth, are ideal for building, carpentry, and cabinetmaking. Woods such as teak, rosewood, and mahogany are valued all over the world for their beauty and durability. Felling and removing the great trees from the rain forest is usually referred to as logging.

A hundred or more years ago, when logging was done with animal power and hand tools, it was a difficult and dangerous business. Loggers were regarded as heroes, brave men that felled giant trees in what was regarded as a hostile environment. Two things changed: logging became mechanized so that it was quicker and safer; and, much later, people came to recognize the value of irreplaceable ancient forests and demand that they be protected. However, the public image of the heroic logger was very difficult to alter. Furthermore, the value of the timber increased as it became rarer, so logging became big business, with huge sums of money involved. Most of today's problems in defending the remaining rain forests arise from the economic value of the timber and the amount of money invested in extracting it from its ancient forest home.

KEY FACTS

● Huge ancient trees produce high-quality timber, worth a lot of money to logging companies.

● Only 6 percent of the world's remaining forests are legally protected.

● Since 1970 about one-fifth of the world's tropical forests have been felled, an area of nearly 2 million sq. mi. (5 million km²).

A view of Vancouver Island, Canada. This whole area was once a temperate rain forest and is a powerful reminder of the damaged caused by clear-cutting.

Modern logging is usually done by clear-cutting, which means cutting down all of the trees in a chosen area so that the ground is left bare. The first task is to make a road into the forest so that machinery can be moved in. Later the logs are dragged to the road and transported out of the forest. The impact of these roads can be severe. Not only do they take up space—about 10 acres per mile (16 ha per km)—but they also compact the soil, increasing runoff and thus erosion. Soil is washed into rivers by rainfall and swept out to sea. On its way, it may kill plants and animals in small streams by turning them into muddy torrents. Sometimes heavy rains cause landslides; huge amounts of soil are washed down the hillside, causing even more damage to the streams and rivers below. Roads also give hunters and poachers access to the deep forest.

Cutting Down a Tree

Once the roads are built, the logging can begin. Felling a large tree, perhaps 200 feet (60 m) or more tall, is a spectacular event. First the loggers use a chain saw to cut a notch at the base of the trunk on the side where it is intended to fall. Driven by powerful gas engines, some modern chain saws have blades as long as 4 feet (1.2 m). Then the loggers cut through the trunk from the other side until the tree falls. A skilled logger can drop a tree within inches of the intended destination, avoiding other trees nearby and leaving it positioned so that it will be as easy as possible to drag it out of the forest.

The job becomes easier as it goes on: the first few trees are dangerous to fell because they crash into others as they come down, often bringing the others

The ITTO

Founded in 1983, the International Tropical Timber Organization (ITTO) was set up to regulate the demand for timber grown in tropical forests and sold on world markets. The ITTO's purpose is to promote sustainable development of tropical forests by encouraging the tropical timber industry and trade to manage and conserve the forests responsibly. Tropical timber-producing members of the ITTO include the Central African Republic, the Congo Republic, the Democratic Republic of the Congo, India, Papua New Guinea, Thailand, Malaysia, Brazil, Colombia, Ecuador, Honduras, Guyana, Suriname, and Venezuela. Consumers of tropical timber are also members of the organization and include the European Union, Canada, and the United States.

The ITTO had hoped to ensure that by the year 2000 all tropical timber products traded internationally would originate from sustainably managed forests. This has not yet been achieved. In 1998, 960 million cu. yd. (735 million m³) of logs were cut down in member states; 15 percent of this was from tropical forests.

down with them in unpredictable directions. Loggers can be injured or even killed at this stage of the work. Later, when it is easier to avoid other trees, the work progresses more quickly and safely.

After the tree has been brought down, loggers run along the massive trunk in spiked boots, deftly removing the branches with their chain saws, making it easier to move. There is no doubt that the operation requires great skill and a lot of courage, with huge side branches crashing to the ground. Then massive machines haul the trunk to the road, using thick steel cables lashed around it. Fitting the cables is another highly skilled and often dangerous part of the job. Sometimes the trunk has to be hauled across a valley on an aerial cable, another spectacular sight. As the work of clear-cutting goes on, the forest is gradually shaved away from the hillside and more roads must be built.

In some countries different methods may be used. In India teak trees are often killed as they stand. The trunk is cut all the way around to break the upward flow of water and nutrients. The tree will then be felled several years later. In Nigeria timber is transported down rivers in floating rafts, a method once used in North American forests. In some Asian countries such as Thailand (where logging is now banned), elephants were used instead of trucks to remove the timber from the forest. The timber may be taken to a sawmill to be cut into planks, or it might be exported as round logs to be processed in some distant country.

When the timber has been hauled away, the remaining branches are burned, leaving the ground bare of trees and covered in ash. The loggers' work is finished.

Environmental Damage

The damage done to the environment by logging is much more than just the removal of the trees. If the cleared area were to be left alone for 100 years or so, the forest would regenerate itself, as it has naturally done for thousands of years—for example, after fires or violent storms.

Giant logging trucks need firm roads on which to carry logs out of the forest. Roads are one of the main causes of damage associated with logging.

Broad buttress roots helped this tree to stand for centuries in the forests of Borneo. They also make cutting down these trees more difficult.

roads and clear-cutting another area of priceless rain forest.

Many rain forest countries owe large amounts of money to more developed Western nations. Because the timber is so valuable, it is very tempting for countries with few other natural resources to fell and export their rain forest trees as quickly as they can to pay their debts. Major timber-exporting countries such as Malaysia and Myanmar find a ready market in wealthy countries where timber is scarce, principally Japan. Thailand was a big exporter until logging was banned in 1989. Cambodia has inflicted serious damage on its rain forests by logging, and in Irian Jaya in Indonesia, large areas of forest were destroyed in the 1960s, along with the way of life of the Asmat (AHZ-maht) people who lived in them. In Africa most of the forests of Cameroon, the Democratic Republic of the Congo, and Gabon were sold off to

However, the roads that loggers build into the forest, often on steep and previously inaccessible hillsides, allow farmers into the area. If people then start cultivating the land, there is no chance for the forest to grow back again. Surveys have shown that every mile of logging road—and probably also farmers occupying the land— causes the deforestation of more than 15 square miles (1 km causes as much as 24 km^2) of what was once forest.

Farmers plant crops, but because of the lack of nutrients under the soil's surface, rain forest land is exhausted after two or three seasons. The farmers then typically sell the land to ranchers, who plant grass and raise cattle for a few years more. When the cattle have trampled the land and eaten all the grass, it is practically useless and may become a virtual desert. Meanwhile, the loggers are busy building

IN FOCUS

Dying Trees

Research in the Amazon has shown that fragmenting rain forests causes damage to large old trees left standing. Large trees within 1,000 ft. (300 m) of the forest edge die three times more quickly than they do when they are surrounded by smaller trees deep within the forest that protect them from exposure to the elements.

Rivers are still used as a means of transporting logs from the rain forests in Indonesia.

Whatever the truth might be, the rate of deforestation by logging is still too fast. Since 1970 about one-fifth of the world's tropical forests have been felled, an area of nearly 2 million square miles (5 million km^2).

logging companies in 1998, including areas close to reserves where rare animals such as the bongo (a kind of antelope) have their last refuge. Indonesia contains 10 percent of the world's forests and 40 percent of those found in Asia. Each year 4,000 square miles (10,500 km^2) are felled, an area twice the size of Delaware. Only Brazil is felling its forests more quickly.

The rate of destruction of the world's tropical rain forests by logging shows little sign of slowing down. In the early 1990s, about 70 acres (28 ha) were being felled every minute, which works out to about 35 million acres (14 million ha) every year. This is less than in the 1980s, when the figure was said to be about 40 million acres (16 million ha) per year. However, the figure for the early 1990s might be wrong because it was based on reports from the Brazilian government that said they had slowed down the rate of clearing forests in the Amazon River basin. Satellite images, however, show that certainly in the late 1990s, the Amazon forests were being cleared just as fast as they had been in the 1980s.

Nearly a third of Asia's tropical forests have been cleared in those 30 years. Only 6 percent of the world's remaining forests are legally protected, leaving more than 12,740,000 square miles (33 million km^2) still at the mercy of logging companies and the needs and decisions of national governments.

Repairing the Damage

It is clearly important to try to extend the area protected by law, but meanwhile conservationists are working to find ways in which timber production can be continued without destroying the entire forest ecosystem. These methods are often called sustainable logging.

One possibility is selective felling, in which individual trees are chosen to extract the best value from the forest without doing too much harm to the environment. This is a good idea, but it has serious drawbacks, mainly because taking out individual trees is as difficult and dangerous as felling the first few trees in a clear-cutting operation. Selective felling also means going into the forest more often, disturbing the wildlife and compacting the ground every time. Where the timber is valuable enough, this may be avoided by lifting it out of the forest with helicopters, but this is very expensive.

Another way of continuing logging without destroying the forests is to replant cleared areas so that companies can harvest a new crop of timber when it is ready, perhaps 20 or 40 or even 100 years later. This too is a good idea, but it does not produce the quality of timber that can be found in ancient rain forests; the planted trees are too young, and in irrigated and fertilized forests, they grow too quickly to have the fine, close grain of older, slow-growing trees. Timber from these plantations is most often used for building or to make chipboard or pulp for paper, not for high-quality carpentry.

Planting new forests does not replace the habitat that was lost when the original forest was felled. An important part of any natural forest habitat is dead trees, where beetles can burrow and woodpeckers can feed on them, with leaf litter full of insects and their predators. Undergrowth and lower-story plants do not grow in a dark new plantation. All these features need time to develop, and some scientists say that it takes as long as 200 years for a forest to become mature.

Logging was once a natural way for humans to make use of forests, when it was done on a small scale and the forests could

be left to regenerate before people returned to make use of them once more. However, since it became a major industry with vast amounts of money involved, it has done nothing but harm the world's forests. Until someone invents a substitute for the beautiful timber that can be produced from tall, ancient trees, the problem of logging will persist.

IN FOCUS

Competitive Logging

Public displays of powerful machinery and spectacular deeds reinforce the image of loggers as heroes. In the temperate rain forest of the Olympic Peninsula, Washington, loggers compete with high-powered chain saws to see who can cut through a large tree quickest.

Check these out:
● Clear-Cutting ● Deforestation
● Exploitation ● Forestry ● Human
Interference ● Tree

Lorises are small animals up to 12 inches (30 cm) long, with round furry faces, moist black noses, large eyes, and round ears. As in humans, their thumbs can be placed opposite to their other fingers for gripping branches. Lorises can also do this with their big toes. The second finger of each hand has a claw instead of a nail, which is used for grooming the fur on its head and neck. The bottom front teeth stick out to form a kind of comb, and are used in grooming and for scooping gum out of cracks in tree bark.

The slow loris and the slender loris live in the rain forests of Asia, and the potto and golden potto (also called the angwantibo) live in the African forests. Their woolly coats range from yellowish gray to golden brown and dark reddish brown, with pale underparts. Only the potto has a visible tail.

Scared Stiff

Lorises and pottos move very slowly along the branches, hand over hand, rather like chameleons. Hunting by night, they use their excellent sense of smell to sniff out slow-moving prey such as beetles and caterpillars. They also eat fruit and the gum that oozes from the trunks of some trees. Although they prefer to eat nice-tasting insects, they will also eat prey that smells or tastes awful, including poisonous millipedes, caterpillars with irritating hairs, and foul-smelling beetles.

If a loris is frightened, it freezes instantly, even if it has one leg in the air. As soon as it stops moving, it becomes very difficult to see in the thick vegetation. It can stay like this for hours until it is sure danger has passed. If extremely frightened, it may drop to the ground. By day it sleeps well hidden in the fork or hollow of a tree.

Surprise Tactics

The potto has a novel form of defense. The bones at the back of its neck and on its back form a series of knobs. The skin covering this bony shield has sensitive hairs up to 4 inches (10 cm) long. If attacked, it buries its head in its hands and directs its shield toward the threat. Clinging firmly to its branch, the potto dodges from side to side, then suddenly straightens out and gives its attacker a nasty bite. Or it may take a swing with its shield, knocking its attacker off the branch.

A slender loris gets a firm grip on a branch. If alarmed, it will freeze its position.

Check these out:

● Mammal ● Nocturnal Animal

Madagascar

Madagascar is the largest island of the African continent and the fourth largest island in the world. It lies in the Mozambique Channel, about 250 miles (400 km) from the African mainland. The north is mountainous, rising to 9,433 feet (2,876 m) above sea level. The wettest region is in the northwest, the driest in the far south. The east coast is generally hot and humid. Most surviving forest lies in the north-eastern part of the island, but some also covers the northwest. Madagascar contains mountain and lowland rain forest, with tangles of mangroves fringing the coast.

The island of Madagascar was isolated from the African mainland about 50 million years ago. Over the ages a vast range of plants and creatures evolved there that were

KEY FACTS

● **Over 1,000 orchid species have been found growing on Madagascar.**

● **Madagascar has about 12,000 species of wild flowering plants. Of these, over 80 percent are unique to the island.**

● **As much as 85 percent of Madagascar's natural tropical forests have been destroyed. Many unique forest animals are now extinct.**

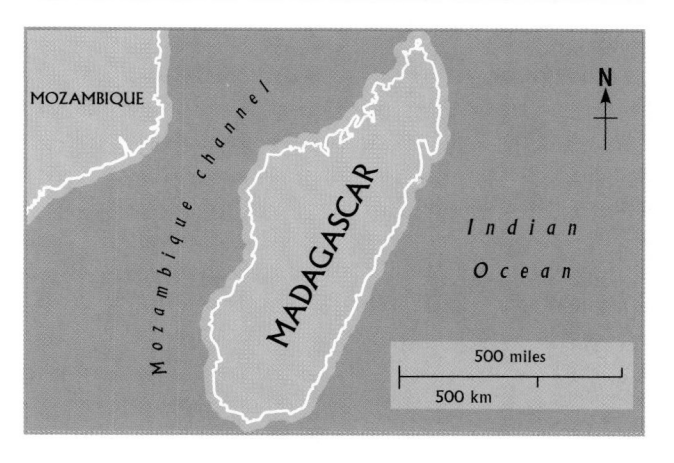

like no others on Earth. Humans first came to live in Madagascar between 2,200 and 1,000 years ago. They were not Africans but Malay-Polynesian seafarers from the Indo-Pacific Ocean region. Later, Arabs, Persians, Africans, and Europeans came to the island. The French explorer Philippe de Comerson, visiting Madagascar in 1771, described it as a "promised land" for naturalists. What impressed him was the island's biodiversity, the extreme variety of species. The island has always been one of the richest natural environments on Earth.

Forest rises amid the Indian Ocean on Nosy Tanikely, an island off the northwest coast of Madagascar.

Madagascar's Lemurs

According to the World Conservation Monitoring Centre, 17 species and subspecies of the lemur (LEE-muhr) family, 5 species of the indri family, and a related creature called the aye-aye (IE-ie) are currently at risk in Madagascar as a result of rain forest destruction. These are all relatives of monkeys and are only found on Madagascar and other smaller islands in the region. Most lemurs are about the size of a cat, but some are tiny. They live in the trees. Some species come out at night to hunt small mammals and insects or to eat tropical fruits.

The Devastation

Throughout history the settlers on Madagascar formed various groups and kingdoms. Madagascar was a French colony from 1896 to 1960, and settlers cleared land for plantations to grow crops such as coffee and for temporary cultivation, using the slash-and-burn method. They brought in humpbacked zebu (ZEE-boo) cattle from the African mainland. More permanent agriculture was introduced for growing rice, which has always formed a large part of the local diet. Logging companies felled tropical hardwoods.

In the years since 1960, these same activities have increased. Crops grown for local use include sweet potatoes, cassavas, and bananas. Other tropical crops grown for export include sugarcane and peanuts. A key crop of the rain forest region is vanilla, an orchid cultivated for its pod,

Rice paddies and terraces occupy a valley that once was densely forested. Rice is an important crop on Madagascar.

which is used in flavoring food and making perfumes.

The island's human population numbers 14.4 million and is increasing at a rate of 2.9 percent each year, placing a huge pressure on the environment. There has been wide-scale logging, charcoal burning (making wood into charcoal, a fuel for cooking stoves), clearing land for agriculture and for pasture, and overgrazing by herds of goats. Cleared forest land can sustain crops for only a year or two, and, if left, is taken over by scrub and forests that lack the original biodiversity and slow-growth hardwood trees.

In many places tropical rains have entirely washed away Madagascar's red soil, leaving barren bedrock where once was one of the world's richest ecosystems. The soil has been washed out to sea, where it is silting up another rich ecosystem, the offshore coral reefs.

The Threat of Extinction

Island wildlife species are always more vulnerable than those of mainland habitats. They have often survived for long ages without predators or competition for their food or nesting sites. When they do come up against danger, there is no easy route of escape off the island.

Human settlement made an early impact on Madagascar's wildlife, with many species becoming extinct as forest was cleared. The island was once home to the world's largest bird, 10 feet (3 m) tall and flightless. European pirates, Arab slave traders, and hungry ships' crews hunted this "elephant bird" for food and collected its massive eggs—35 inches (90 cm) around the shell—as curiosities. By about 1700 it was extinct. In 1920, a large rain forest cuckoo called Delalande's Madagascar coucal also became extinct.

It has been estimated that 127 species of animals remain at risk on Madagascar today, including 46 mammals, 27 birds, and 13 reptiles. The aye-aye is one of the most endangered species. Bred in foreign zoos, it has been reintroduced to the offshore island of Nosy Mangabe.

Changing Direction

Madagascar will never again be a "promised land:" it has gone too far down the road of human development. However, since the 1980s, the world has woken up to the importance of biodiversity, and Madagascar has become a prime site for conservation work by botanists and zoologists.

Scientific research sites, forest stations, reserves, and national parks have been created to protect the island's surviving

The red–ruffed lemur is an endangered species. Its survival may depend on captive breeding programs.

habitats. The most recently created is the Masaola National Park, covering 840 square miles (2,175 km^2) of a peninsula in the island's northeast. It includes the rain forest itself, which has an astonishing variety of palm species, as well as offshore coral reefs. The forest there has long been under threat from loggers, local farmers, and villagers collecting firewood. Now there is some hope that its rarest inhabitants—the Madagascar red owl and the red-ruffed lemur—will survive, against all the odds.

Check these out:
- Biodiversity ● Deforestation
- Endangered Species ● Erosion ● Lemur

Makah People

The Makah (muh-KAW) are a native people of the North American temperate rain forest. They live on the Pacific Coast of the Olympic Peninsula in the state of Washington.

Taking to the Sea

To take advantage of the mild climate and rich resources, the Makahs built their villages on the coast. The Pacific currents there are abundant in fish and marine mammals.

Neah Bay, on Cape Flattery, is the largest Makah community. During the 1700s and 1800s, Spanish, Russian, British, and American ships visited frequently. One ship, in 1853, carried smallpox, which reduced the Makah population from about 2,000 people to around 500. During the 1990s the group's population was about 1,000.

A people of the sea, the Makahs have been the only Native American people in North America to protect their whaling rights in treaties with the United States. An international whaling commission has allotted the Makah the harvesting of two whales each year. That ruling brought protests by animal rights groups. In 1998 and 1999, environmental protesters attempted to prevent the Makahs from putting out to sea in their whaling canoes.

Until the Makahs had stopped hunting whales more than a century ago, they were notorious for their courage in paddling their small, eight-man canoes far out to sea to harpoon whales, which was very dangerous. The whales would

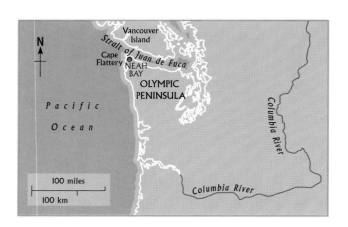

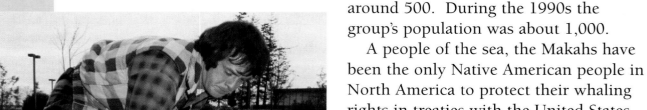

The Makahs are skilled at fashioning objects from red cedar trees taken from the rain forest.

350

IN FOCUS

Uncovering the Past

Between 300 and 500 years ago, a mud slide buried the Makah village of Ozette. In 1970 the village was discovered in nearly perfect condition under the mud. Makahs worked with scientists to recover a wealth of artifacts and built the Makah Cultural and Research Center to house them. The studies helped spark a revival of Makah culture and language.

approaching manhood would seek a remote part of the forest to fast and seek a vision quest, a spiritual experience. Makah healers ventured deep into the rain forest to harvest plants and herbs for treating illnesses. The knowledge of the healing properties of many rain forest plants was handed down from generation to generation, a store of knowledge built up for unknown centuries. Today the Makah people are experiencing a revival of their traditional customs and learning.

be buoyed up with skin floats and towed back to shore.

Commercial fishing is now an important part of the Makah economy. Artisans also harvest olivella shells from their beaches to make jewelry. The Makah have also converted the abandoned naval air station at Cape Flattery into a resort for tourists.

The Makahs and their Rain Forest

The Makah Reservation was established by treaty in 1855. Today it has 27,000 acres (11,000 ha). The Makah Tribal Council oversees important areas of tribal life, including law enforcement, labor relations, fishing interests, tribal enrollment, and the leasing of tribal resources and properties. Clear-cutting of their ancient forests by large logging companies poses a major problem.

For the Makahs the red cedar tree provides a crucial rain forest resource. Women harvest cedar bark, soak it in water, and pound it to make it soft and then fashion skirts and blankets with it. The men selectively harvest the cedar for making canoes.

In Makah traditional life, the rain forest was a place where teenage boys

Many items from Makah traditional life were recovered when their village of Ozette was excavated. It had been buried by a mud slide between 300 and 500 years ago.

Check these out:

- Disease • People of the Rain Forest
- Temperate Rain Forest

Mammal

There are signs of mammals everywhere in the rain forest. The rain forest is full of the noisy calls of monkeys chasing each other through the treetops and the alarm calls of other mammals when they spot a snake or other threat. On the ground are the prints of deer, rodents, cats, and other creatures; the torn and chewed remains of their meals; and their droppings. Less obvious are the narrow paths leading through the forest made by deer or the burrows of armadillos, foxes, mice, and voles.

Mammals are animals that feed their young on milk secreted by their mothers from special glands called mammae (hence the name *mammals*). In most mammals the young suck milk from special nipples on their mother's belly. Most mammals' young are born small and helpless and need their mother's care until they can fend for themselves. Mammals are usually covered in hair or fur.

A leaf-nosed bat flies in to feed. Its large wings are supported by very long fingers.

Another unique feature is the palate—the roof of the mouth—that separates the nose from the mouth so that mammals can breathe while they eat.

Mammals vary in size from the largest elephant, which can stand at 8 feet (2.5 m) at the shoulder and weigh around 11,000 pounds (5,000 kg), to the smallest, Kitti's hog-nosed bat, which lives in limestone caves on the Kwae Noi (the Kwai River) in southwestern Thailand and weighs between .06 and .07 ounces (1.7 to 2 grams).

Like birds, mammals are warm-blooded, which means that they can generate their own body heat and do not depend on their surroundings for warmth. Mammals breed at a slower rate than many other animals. In the rain forest, where food of all kinds is abundant year round, many mammals do not wait for a particular season: they breed when the opportunity arises at any time of year.

A Tiny Possum

Australia's tiny honey possum feeds almost exclusively on nectar. Such a specialized diet is possible only in tropical rain forests, where trees flower all year round. An adult male's body length is 2 1/2 to 3 1/3 in. (6.5 to 8.5 cm), while an adult female can be up to 3 1/2 in. (9 cm) long.

young develop inside their mother's womb, attached to her body by a fleshy structure called the placenta. Inside the placenta the baby's blood vessels mingle with its mother's, absorbing oxygen and nutrients and getting rid of waste. These babies are born in a more advanced state than the marsupial babies, but many placental mammals are still born naked, blind, and helpless.

Eggs, Pouches, and Placentas

There are three main groups of mammals. The strangest are the egg-laying mammals, or monotremes, found only in Australia and nearby regions. The spiny anteater, or echidna (ih-KID-nuh), probes the ground for ants and termites with its long, hairless snout. The female echidna lays a single egg, which she keeps warm in a special pouch on her belly. When the tiny young hatches, naked and blind, it laps up milk that oozes out through a patch of skin on her belly.

The second group of mammals is the pouched mammals, or marsupials. Newborn marsupials are incredibly tiny, more like little naked embryos—they weigh less than 1 gram (0.04 oz). However, their front limbs are strong enough to claw their way through their mother's fur to her abdomen, where they can cling to one of her nipples, or teats. In many marsupials the mother carries the babies in a pouch or marsupium. Rain forest marsupials include the American opossums and the tree kangaroos, forest wallabies, possums, and bandicoots of Australia and New Guinea.

All other mammals, including humans, are placental mammals: the

Flexible Feet

All mammals that live on land have feet with five toes, but there the similarity ends. Like humans, monkeys have opposable thumbs (and often big toes as well). This helps them grasp branches and enables them to grip and manipulate objects. Otters, capybaras, and platypuses have webbed feet for swimming. Moles dig underground tunnels with their huge curved claws, while anteaters and aardvarks

The mouse opossum, which inhabits Central and South American forests, is a marsupial that does not have a pouch.

use theirs to tear open termite and ant nests. Many cats can draw their claws back into a sheath when they are trying to sneak up on prey, then extend them to slash at the prey or to climb trees. The aye-aye (IE-ie) has a long, thin claw on its middle finger for digging grubs out of crevices in bark.

Mammals in the Food Web

Mammals thrive at most levels of the rain forest food web. Most of the top predators that roam the forest are mammals—the panthers, jaguars, tigers, and leopards. There are other predators, too: smaller cats, foxes, and bats that chase insects through the canopy at night, shrews that seize them in the undergrowth,

and anteaters, armadillos, and pangolins that eat ants and termites. These mammals are all carnivores, or flesh eaters. Their teeth are sharp and pointed. Many of them also use sharp claws on their toes to cling to their prey or rip its flesh. The smaller hunters that feed on insects—the insectivores such as shrews and bats—tend to have more uniform teeth, also with sharp points, for crushing the hard shells of insects.

A few carnivores hunt underwater. Found throughout the Tropics, otters propel their sleek, streamlined bodies through the water with their powerful tails, using their webbed feet to steer.

There are even mammals that hunt in the air. The hordes of insects that thrive in the moist rain forest provide food for many different bats, from the large flying foxes of Asia to the tiny tent bats that live in folded leaves in the rain forests of Central and South America.

A Variety of Vegetarians

Carnivorous mammals prey on the vegetarians—the rabbits, bandicoots, bears, sloths, deer, and gorillas that feed exclusively on plants. The warm, steamy rain forests are home to the greatest diversity of plant-eating mammals on the planet. Secretive and seldom seen, sloths live in the rain forests of Central and South America. Hanging upside down from branches, they slowly munch their way through the toughest leaves. On the other side of the world, tree kangaroos feed in the treetops, while forest wallabies graze in forest glades. Squirrels

Genets

Genets (JEH-nuhts), members of the mongoose family from Africa and the Mediterranean region, have pointed snouts, long furry tails, and large ears. They hunt at night in the trees, stalking mice, rats, and birds. Seldom seen, many species have striking, patterned coats.

The white-nosed coati (kuh-WAH-tee) of Central and South America is the ultimate omnivore, foraging in the trees and on the ground for anything from fruits to eggs, insects, and mice.

Omnivores

In between the predators and the vegetarians are the omnivores—eaters of everything, or almost everything. Many mammals eat a wide range of food whenever and wherever they find it. Monkeys will flock to trees that are producing fruit or to feast on the nectar from masses of flowers, but they will also eat small mammals, eggs, and insects.

Herds of peccaries charge through the forests of Central and South America, using their snouts and hooves to dig down to roots, fungi, and worms and churning up the forest floor in search of fallen fruits and nuts. Wild pigs and hogs live in other tropical forests.

In the rain forests of North and South America, some of the greatest opportunists are the raccoon and the coati. Bold and inquisitive, the raccoon will even venture inside houses in search of delicacies. Coatis have similar tastes to raccoons, and both can climb trees. The American opossums and the Australian bandicoots and possums like to mix their fruits and vegetables with insects for variety.

Bears are also omnivores. South America's spectacled bear will eat the juicy hearts of bromeliads, palm stalks, and figs. It will also feed on carrion (animal carcasses), insects, and even small mammals. The Asian sun bear has a similar diet and sometimes catches birds, too.

thrive in tropical rain forests worldwide, feasting on young shoots, fruits, and nuts.

On the forest floor, small herds of deer graze on the bushes. In South America the capybara feeds on grasses along riverbanks and even in streams and lakes, while around tropical shores and estuaries, manatees spend their whole lives underwater nibbling on aquatic plants.

In dense African rain forests, okapis use their long neck and muscular tongue to pull down shoots from forest trees. The tapirs of Central and South America and Asia have long, flexible snouts, which they wrap around shoots to pull them off. However, the experts at this game are the forest elephants. A few herds of African elephants live in tropical forests, and many Indian elephants are at home there. Their trunks are powerful enough to pull down small trees, or they can use their massive heads to push them down.

Love Potions

Mammals often communicate by scent. Chemicals called pheromones are produced from glands under the tail and on the thighs, feet, cheeks, and elsewhere, depending on the species. Often the scents tell other members of the species about their identity and sex and whether they are ready to mate. More scents may be produced in the urine or droppings. Members of the cat and dog families spray scented urine on tree stumps and bushes to tell other animals where their territory is. Tree shrews urinate on their paws, marking the tree bark where they walk; and deer rub scent from glands below their eyes.

A tree shrew feeds on a rafflesia flower in Sumatra. Tree shrews also feed on insects, fruit, and small mammals.

Homes and Hiding Places

The rain forest offers many hiding places. Mice, voles, rabbits, foxes, and badgers make their homes in burrows in the forest floor. Raccoons, galagos, and many other small mammals find safety inside hollow trees, often lining them with leaves for comfort. Gorillas make nests of leaves and branches wherever they stop to rest, in the fork of a tree or on the ground. The sloth relies on not moving to conceal itself. With a coat almost the color of its surroundings and casting no shadow on the branch because it hangs below it, it is extremely difficult to spot.

Social Life

While most of the rain forest's hunters live solitary lives, many of the vegetarians and scavengers live in groups. With a group of animals on the lookout, they can more easily find new fruits or nuts fallen to the ground or trees that are bursting with new tender shoots. Deer often live in single-sex groups outside the breeding season, but when mating time comes the males compete for harems of females.

Mice and voles live alone, but pigs tend to live in small groups—a female and her young or a bunch of bachelors. Old males often prefer their own company. Peccaries, by contrast, live in herds of up to 100 individuals. Monkeys and apes live in complex social groups dominated by a large, powerful male. Groups defend a home territory from other groups, usually by ritualized calling and threat displays but sometimes by bloody fights. Keeping a territory ensures that the group has enough to eat.

Check these out:

● Ape ● Bat ● Bear ● Carnivore ● Cat
● Food Web ● Galago ● Herbivore
● Mongoose ● Possum ● Primate

Manatees are large mammals that live in shallow coastal areas, estuaries, and rivers along tropical coasts. Often called sea cows, they spend their whole lives underwater, feeding on aquatic plants. Occasionally they come to the surface to take a fresh breath.

Shaped like a stout torpedo, the manatee has no hind legs. Its front legs form flippers, and there is also a flipper at its tail end. Its head is small, with little eyes and a square, bristly snout. Manatees grow up to 15 feet (4.5 m) long and may weigh 1,500 pounds (700 kg).

There are three species of manatees: West African, West Indian, and Amazonian. Another sea cow, the dugong, is found from the southwest Pacific Ocean to the coast of eastern Africa. The Amazonian manatee has a pinkish belly patch, while the other species are a fairly uniform gray.

Manatees move very slowly unless they are in danger. They use their tail fin to propel themselves and their front flippers for steering. A thick layer of blubber (fat) keeps them warm and also serves as a food store.

Plant fibers wear down manatees' peglike teeth. To cope with this, manatees have a unique conveyor belt of teeth: the teeth move forward slowly in the jaw; as they wear down, they are replaced by new teeth from the back of the jaw.

Manatees sometimes appear to be kissing. This action is used to reinforce bonding between members of a group, though manatees do not have a strong social organization. They have no vocal cords, but they communicate using high-pitched squeaks and chirps.

Manatees spend their entire lives underwater, browsing on aquatic plants. They are the sloths of the underwater world.

Endangered Manatees

Manatees everywhere are under threat. In some places people hunt them for food, their skins, and the oil from their blubber. However, many countries now protect them by law since they perform a valuable service by keeping waterways clear of vegetation. Modern threats include dams, pollution, and boat traffic: boat propellers often seriously injure manatees. Manatees breed very slowly—a female may live for 50 years yet produce only six young—so it is hard for them to recover from damage to their environment or to their species.

Check these out:

● Herbivore ● Mammal ● River

Glossary

Bacteria: microscopic single-celled organisms. Bacteria are usually smaller than the cells of other organisms.

Bromeliad: short-stemmed plants with a rosette of overlapping concave leaves in which water may collect. Some bromeliads grow on the forest floor, but many are epiphytes.

Camouflage: disguise that works to deceive a predator or prey animal.

Carbon dioxide: a gas that makes up less than one part per thousand of the air around us. It is essential for plants because they cannot make their food without it.

Chitin: a hard, horny substance found in the outer skeleton (exoskeleton) or "shell" of invertebrates and in the cell walls of fungi. It is tough but flexible and is a combination of a protein and a carbohydrate.

Cilia: threadlike organs that project out from the body of a cell.

Cuticle: the outer layer of an organism. It is usually made up of dead cells impregnated with waterproofing waxes and a tough substance like chitin (invertebrates) or keratin (vertebrates) that also helps prevent the entry of bacteria and fungi.

Deciduous: deciduous trees are those that drop all of their leaves at a certain time of year.

Epiphyte: any plant that grows on another without taking any food from it. Most epiphytes grow on trees, and they are very common in the rain forest. They include many ferns and orchids.

Fauna: all the kinds of animals from a particular area.

Flora: all the kinds of living plants, including flowering plants, ferns, and mosses, from a particular area.

Herbaceous: plants that have soft stems with no woody component.

Invertebrate: an animal that lacks a spinal column (backbone). Invertebrates may have a hard outer shell, like insects.

Leishmaniasis: a group of three different diseases that are caused by different parasites, and that are transmitted to humans by sandfly bites.

Mangrove: any one of many kinds of shrubs and trees that grow in muddy tidal areas along coasts and up tidal rivers, mainly in the Tropics. Many mangroves send down aerial roots from their branches into the mud below. These roots are specially adapted to cope with the salt water that swamps them at high tide.

Marsupial: a mammal whose young are born very small and helpless after a brief pregnancy, and that complete their development attached to their mother's teats, usually in a pouch called a marsupium.

Microbe: a microscopic organism too small to see with the naked eye.

Nectar: a sweet, sugar-rich scented liquid produced by flowers to attract insects for pollination.

Nymph: the immature stage of a variety of insects that undergo a simple metamorphosis from young to adult form. The nymph is generally similar to the adult and does not pass through a pupal stage to get to its adult state.

Peninsula: an area of land almost completely surrounded by water that is attached to a larger area of land.

Photosynthesis: the process by which green plants combine water and carbon dioxide from the air to make simple sugars, which they use as energy-giving food.

Placenta: an organ that develops in many mammals to link a developing fetus to its mother's womb.

Poacher: a person who hunts animals that are protected by law, or one who hunts on land belonging to someone else.

Pollen: microscopic dustlike spores produced by seed-bearing plants. They contain the male sex cells, and when they land on another flower of the same species, they release these cells to fertilize it.

Primate: any type of mammal with a relatively large brain, hands and feet that can grasp things (often with opposable thumbs or big toes), usually five fingers and toes with flattened nails instead of claws, and good eyesight.

Spore: a tiny, dustlike reproductive cell produced by mosses, liverworts, ferns, and fungi. It eventually grows into a new plant.

Staple food: the main, usually starchy, food eaten by a group of people.

Starch: a complex chemical that provides the main food storage cells in plants. Many human foodstuffs are made from the starches of plants such as potatoes and grains.

Ultraviolet: a kind of radiation just beyond the violet end of the light spectrum. It is present in sunlight but invisible to human eyes. Many animals, such as insects, can see it.

Index

360